Benjamin   George   Maria

Sloop

Schooner

Dogger

Swift   Phoenix   Amy   Hope

Ketch

With very best wishes on your visit to Poole.

Josiah Beaumont 10th November 1990

Mansions and Merchants of Poole and Dorset

by

Derek Beamish   John Hillier   H F V Johnstone

designed by Graham Smith

Volume One

Poole Historical Trust
Poole 1976

This volume is published by the Poole Historical Trust whose primary aims
are the promotion of research into and the publication of works on the history and
life of Poole and the surrounding area.

Previous Publications

The Pride of Poole 1688–1851
1974 (out of Print)

An Album of Old Poole
1975

Photographs
Copyright Poole Historical Trust & Poole Museums Service 1976
Photography and photographic copying by Chris Hart
Printed by Southbourne Printing Co Ltd
Bound by Kemp Hall Bindery, Oxford

Acknowledgements

We are grateful for the loan of documents and for help in our research to:

Poole Corporation; Poole Museums Service;
Dorset County Reference Libraries at Poole and Dorchester;
Dorset County Museum; Dorset County Record Office;

Mr A Coates; Mrs C W Douie and Mr K Mc C Douie;
Miss E M Lester-Garland; Sir Thomas Lees, Bart;
Professor Keith Matthews of the Memorial University, Newfoundland;
Mr D Owens, St John's, Newfoundland; Mr Andrew Pearce;
Mrs Bobbie Robertson of the Newfoundland Historical Society;
Mrs E J Shepard; Mr K A P Smith;
and our many correspondents in Poole, Dorset, Newfoundland and the USA.

We are also grateful to those who have helped in the past to keep
alive an interest in the history of Poole, its people and trade, notably the late
H P Smith, Herbert S Carter, Bernard Short and more recently Dr E F J Matthews
and many others.

Contents

List of Illustrations and Maps

Preface

In the following pages we have told the stories of some of the merchants who were Poole people or men who came from Dorset, Hampshire or Somerset who, trading out of the port of Poole in their small sailing ships, established a successful commerce with the European ports, the North American colonies and, more importantly and lastingly, in the fisheries of Newfoundland.

This trading lasted from Elizabethan times up to about the middle of the Nineteenth century. Poole's share of this trade varied from decade to decade but, in the more prosperous period starting in the later 1700's and lasting till about 1820, Poole had the lion's share of the Newfoundland trade of the 'Western Adventurers'. Most of the rest of the trade then belonged to the South Devon ports, notably Dartmouth.

Dartmouth has at least the Naval College as a monument to its involvement in this trade and its part in the establishment of the Royal Navy. The only monuments to the successful commerce of the Western Adventurers in Poole and the surrounding areas are the surviving mansions built by the merchants of Poole for their families to live in.

For the most part we have written the history of those of the merchants who are related to the various mansions which they built or bought and which still exist today. In doing so, we have sometimes continued the history of the house, even if its subsequent occupants were unconnected with Poole's trade. At other times, we have followed the history of the merchant's family after it had foresaken the family mansion, and sometimes we have done both. In addition, we have told the history of one mansion which, in a sense, all the merchants owned jointly, that of the Rectory of St James Church.

The choice of the families and of the mansions dealt with in this volume was not entirely premeditated. At first we thought that we could deal in one book with at least all the merchants whose mansions were still extant. It was only when we came to research the history of the merchants, their families and their houses that we found they could not be contained in one volume. We hope to complete the history of the Jolliffes, the Slades and the other merchants in a subsequent book.

We have been most impressed by the great interest shown by many people in Newfoundland, Canada and the USA whose ancestors emigrated out of the port of Poole. We have therefore added vignettes of a few of our correspondents which we are sure will interest everyone – and might even connect parts of very long-separated families!

Introduction

Although there were prominent Poole merchants whose commerce was with places other than Newfoundland, such as the Jolliffes and Thompsons who were mainly concerned with the trade with the North American colonies, Poole's fame and its merchants' fortunes rested mainly on the Newfoundland trade.

The only substantial markets for the dried, salted cod, the staple product of the Newfoundland trade, were in Spain, Portugal and Italy. Thus neither Poole nor Dartmouth, the main home ports of the trade, ever saw the bulk of the produce of their merchants and men in the Newfoundland trade.

The home ports therefore avoided the problems of distribution, but the merchants had plenty of other difficulties to contend with. The ships sailing out of Poole had for centuries in the trade to be provided with everything that was needed to get the ship and the men to Newfoundland, to maintain them there for at least three months, to equip them for their fishing and for the curing of the fish, as well as to get the men and the fish and oil safely back to Europe.

For the ships' provisioning, Poole had its brewers, bakers, candlemakers, and for their victualling there were the daily supplies of meat from Blandford and vegetables from Ringwood. There were, too, adequate supplies of swanskin cloth from Sturminster Newton and other local towns to provide the clothing for the armies of men who left each Spring for the Newfoundland fishing season.

The only provisions which were not readily available in Poole were butter, salted pork, the salt itself and rum. The vessels called at Waterford or Cork en route to Newfoundland where they picked up their supplies of butter and salted pork (and in later periods many immigrants for Newfoundland). The supply of salt required for the curing of the fish in Newfoundland was conveniently available in Spain or Portugal at or near the main markets for the dried fish. Rum was brought back from the West Indies by the vessels taking the cured fish there, a trade which, up to 1775, was mainly carried out by the American settlers.

For ship-building and the repair and refitting of vessels, Poole had its shipwrights, sailmakers, ropemakers, carpenters, blacksmiths, whitesmiths, anchorsmiths, block makers, pump makers and the rest. To ensure supplies of linen cloth the merchants even established their own flax mills locally at Lytchett and Organford. It was the availability of all these services and supplies which drew merchants to Poole from the surrounding districts of Dorset, Hampshire and Somerset. It was, too, these same counties which provided most of the mariners and fishermen for the trade. It was only if the merchant wished to trade in other commodities that he was tempted to take his business to another port.

But there were many other problems for the merchants of Poole. There were the inevitable hazards of the Atlantic crossing in their vessels which, even in the later periods of the trade, rarely exceeded 250 tons. Even when the vessels had reached Newfoundland waters they were still at risk for, even if those seas were free of ice, they were still subject to blinding fogs and great storms as well as sudden violent squalls. Moreover, those seas, as well as those of the Western Approaches to Europe, were frequently haunted by privateers licensed by the countries with which Britain was so frequently at war, and sometimes by outright pirates such as the Barbary pirates of North Africa.

One of the worst of the periods of attacks by privateers was that which covers part of the career of all the families of merchants with whom we deal. That was the period between 1739 and 1815 when the Spanish, French and American privateers captured dozens of the Poole ships. As a result many hundreds of the mariners and fishermen of Dorset, Hampshire and Somerset languished in the prisons of Coruna, Brest and other foreign ports, hoping for the eventual ransom or exchange for foreigners captured by the English.

Success on the fishing grounds was itself subject to the vagaries of the sea currents which affected the route the fish would take, and even good catches did not always guarantee large profits. Prices might be low, markets could suddenly be closed by a declaration of war, or made impossible by the sudden imposition of import duties.

However, of all the problems of the merchants, possibly the most intractable and frustrating to them and their mariners was that of the Press, the method of manning the Royal Navy by compelling trained mariners to man the vessels of the Navy. The Newfoundland fishery was the pre-eminent 'Nursery of seamen'. The mariners, trained in seamanship in the Atlantic and Newfoundland waters formed the back-bone of the Royal Navy and were quite indispensable to it in time of war from the days of Elizabeth right up into Victoria's reign.

These periodic forced enlistments of trained men from the merchants' ships into the Royal Navy were often substantial and serious despite the efforts of the Poole and Dartmouth merchants to foil the hated Press Gangs. Unfortunately, the seasonal nature of the fishing in Newfoundland (for the fish only appeared there in Spring) meant that the mariners came home each autumn. This made the job of the Press easier and led in turn to mariners skipping ship as it returned home at times when 'the Press was hot', leaving the merchants and their captains in trouble with the port authorities for the mariners' disappearance before the vessel had been cleared.

Another bugbear of the merchants was that, if it was suspected that war might occur while the ships were at sea or in Newfoundland, the Government would issue Embargo Warrants. These Warrants prohibited any ships sailing out of the ports until cleared by the Royal Navy and were to ensure that the men required were obtained by the Navy before they had sailed. The Embargo sometimes resulted in a whole fishing season being lost.

Despite all the problems, however, there was always the great incentive for the merchants that a successful period of fishing and trading could give very large rewards. In fact they were sometimes so great that the more successful merchants were sometimes called 'Merchant Princes'.

But those merchants who had reached such an elevated status knew only too well that for as long as they remained in the trade there were far too many rocks, both real and metaphorical, on which their fortunes could founder for them ever to feel their wealth was secure. It was therefore not surprising that many merchants thought of transferring at least a part of their wealth into the more stable ownership of land and of achieving the more elevated social standing of the landed gentry and of encouraging their sons to enter the professions.

Some of the merchants, like the Garlands, succeeded or partially succeeded in doing this, but more failed completely, like the Spurriers, who were overcome by calamity before they could make good their escape from the gamble of the Newfoundland trade.

Other families struggled on manfully in the trade, trying to accommodate their business to the changing times, such as the Slades who for a time did so well in pioneering the seal oil trade in the more northerly waters of Newfoundland and Labrador, and in the import of timber from Quebec. Others, like the Hodges from Crewkerne in Somerset, simply left their base in Poole to live and work in Newfoundland as so many thousands of mariners and tradesmen of Poole and the West of England had done before them.

It was against this background that the merchants built their mansions and lived their lives, some of which we have told in these pages.

Spurrier

Llewellin

Tichborne

PUGNA PRO PATRIA

Upton House

Upton House was built about 1816 by Christopher Spurrier whose family had grown rich on the fat profits of the Newfoundland trade in the 18th and early 19th centuries. Like many of the merchant families who had flourished in this way, the Spurriers appear to have come to Poole, possibly from Wareham, sometime in the 1600's. In 1690 Walter Spurrier was living in Fish Street in a house which formed part of his wife's inheritance; he had indeed married well, for his wife Mary Beale was the daughter of a former mayor of the town and could trace her descent and her property back to Elizabethan days and the trading successes of Nicholas Carey of Fish Street and Upton Farm.

By this time, however, Fish Street was no longer what it had been, and few people of rank or wealth chose to live there; the decaying Guildhall over the town's insecure prison, then almost always propped up by scaffolding, was hardly an attractive feature in the street in which there were also numerous warehouses containing the products of the Newfoundland and associated trades, dried cod, oil from cod, seal and whale, seal skins and blubber. These items in a hot summer or if carelessly handled, could easily become a 'great nuisance to ye inhabitants by reason of ye stench'. They were nonetheless vital to the economic health of the community and Poole merchants frequently corresponded with the government to ensure that they gained whatever favours and assistance government could provide for their trade in these goods. In 1729, for example, the Mayor wrote a spirited letter to the Commissioners for Trade and Plantations protesting at attempts by the Customs authorities to collect duty on oil produced in Newfoundland. Three years later, the Corporation and the merchants were up in arms about the privileges granted to the Greenland fisheries and were able to secure the same advantages for their own trade in whale fins, oil and blubber.

"The trade of Newfoundland", said the Poole merchants in their petition "answers all the beneficial purposes of employing great numbers of seamen and ships, and consuming great quantities of provisions and other British manufactures in a much greater degree than the trade of Greenland."

Whatever the shortcomings of their house in Fish Street, Walter Spurrier and his sons were nonetheless well placed to join in the recovery and later growth in the town's share of the Newfoundland trade which came with the end of the long wars with France. Starting as seamen in the Newfoundland fishing ships of Poole they rose to be captains of these ships and had graduated into the trade as merchants by the early 1720's. The British Government had used their victory over the French in the War of the Spanish Succession to appropriate all the French land in Newfoundland. By the Treaty of Utrecht in 1713 the French colony of Placentia and the whole of the land held by the French in Newfoundland were ceded to the British; in fact only English and Irish people were allowed to set up fishing 'rooms' in Newfoundland. The Spurriers chose to set up their business on the previously French coast at St Mary's Bay in the south of the Avalon Peninsula, well away from most of the Poole merchants whose traditional grounds were further north in Trinity, Bonavista and Conception Bays. The Spurriers were well rewarded for their pioneering spirit in moving into this area for they found they could catch fish earlier than their distant fellow merchants in waters which were less troubled by ice.

It seems likely that the real founder of the family's fortunes was Walter's son Timothy who, born in 1672, had become a member of the great City Company of Merchant Taylors and was elected to the Corporation of Poole in 1719. He rose very quickly to become Mayor in 1722, and to serve again in 1725 and 1730-1. As Mayor, Timothy Spurrier did his best to enforce the fire precautions of his day and instructed the Town Crier to "cry for people to put water at their doors and not to smoak tobacco in ye streets or ye Key". Another announcement of this time, reminding the populace not to break windows (especially those in the Town Hall and the School) and not to shoot in their gardens, indicated how dangerous life in the town could then be. There was even danger in the graveyard for one intriguing entry in Timothy's accounts records the payment of one shilling and sixpence to George Parsons and his son "for burying ye man who was supposed to be buried alive." 1730 and 1731 provide further interesting evidence of Mayor Spurrier's duties: he entertained an important foreign visitor at the Antelope – the Prince of Lebanon, and dispensed charity – sixpence "to a man brought from Newfoundland with no feet"; one shilling "to a cripl'd black," and ninepence "to a man with ye lepersy." In the same year Mayor Spurrier was responsible for a minor change in the administration of the Corporation's finances; hitherto the Town Sergeant, George Savage, who carried out the frequent sentences of whipping passed on miscreants, had been paid separately for each whipping, but from 1730 onwards this aptly named officer was to receive "his whipping salary" of £1 per annum.

Timothy Spurrier was clearly a man of talent to have been chosen as Mayor so quickly and on so many occasions. When he died in 1756 a local newspaper referred to one of his particular qualities and said that "he was so remarkably temperate in his drinking that it is generally said of him that he was never intoxicated with liquor, although he arrived at the age of 84 years." From what is known of the drinking habits of the 18th century men in general, and those of Poole and Newfoundland in particular, this was indeed an unusual distinction!

It did not take long for more of the Spurriers to rise into the small group of men who controlled the town at this time. By 1747 there were six members of the family in the Corporation, including a second Timothy, son of the first, who was now to serve as mayor in 1747 and 1751. During his first Mayoralty 30 new members were admitted to the Corporation to raise money for the repair of the streets and the

Burin Harbour, Newfoundland, one of the finest harbours in the island
and the centre of the Spurrier's business there.

Quay, and to introduce more of their relatives and friends to the Corporation, but Mayor Spurrier, as was customary then, secured the election of his own son, William Spurrier, without paying the then normal fee of £20. By 1751 the Corporation was again short of money and 24 new members were recruited, although on this occasion no members of the Spurrier family were available or thought fit to be elected to the governing body of the town.

The mid-century saw the beginning of dramatic changes for the Newfoundland fisheries. Just as the demand in Europe increased the cod fish themselves appeared off Newfoundland in much greater numbers and the Spurriers, like their fellow Poole merchants, became more prosperous than ever. The family's wealth in the 1760's and 70's was not so great as that amassed by the richest merchants of the town—the Whites, Lesters, Jefferys, Nicklesons, Greens and Pikes – but the will of Timothy Spurrier's widow, Ann, shows that by 1765 the Spurriers had already accumulated much property. Her son, Christopher received her share in the family's town house while her grandson inherited her husband's property in Wareham. One daughter, Mary, became the owner of a house in Market Street formerly occupied by Timothy Spurrier (Junior) and another house let to the town clerk, William Humfrey, passed to her other daughter, Ann. The Spurriers were by this time clearly connected with the extensive Jolliffe family in Poole; members of the family had commanded ships belonging to William Jolliffe, the wealthy merchant in the South Carolina trade, and Peter Jolliffe the younger was now to be an executor of Ann Spurrier's will.

The Spurriers profited too from the misfortunes of other merchant houses. Professor Keith Matthews has pointed out that many of the firms in the Newfoundland trade disappeared when the male line in the families died out, or when the heirs of merchants had no interest in remaining in the trade. When this happened, other established merchants sometimes took over the business of their former fellow merchants. This fate overtook the large Poole firm of Waldren and Young late in the 18th century. Waldren and Young was itself the result of an amalgamation of two of the oldest established Poole firms in Newfoundland. Capt Young, when he established himself as a merchant in 1636 was the first Poole fishing captain to turn merchant. The Clarkes of Poole had begun their merchant business around 1700, and the heirs of these two merchants had later formed the business of Clarke & Young. The mainstream of the Clarke family then died out and Robert Young had taken over the firm; on his death in 1775, William Waldren, previously the resident agent in Newfoundland for Clarke & Young, had taken over the combined firm, then known as Waldren & Young. Waldren & Young were in very large business on the south coast of Newfoundland. When William Waldren himself died, it was William Spurrier who took over Waldren & Young. He was thus able to combine in his own business house three of the largest Newfoundland firms listed by the Naval Officer of Newfoundland in 1785, for the two firms combined in Waldren & Young had both previously qualified for inclusion, one at Oderin and Burin and the other in Fortune Bay.

The Atlantic of Poole in Naples Harbour.
A vessel of 135 tons, she was one of the types commonly used in the Newfoundland trade.

Extract from the Star newspaper of 31 July 1807 concerning William Spurrier's appearance at the bar of the House of Commons.

There was no question now of remaining in the inconvenient Fish Street house and William Spurrier was soon to be found with the Lesters, the Westons and the Slades in Thames Street. Like other Poole merchants too he began to move in fashionable society, and it was at Vauxhall near London that he and his wife were relieved of £12 and their watches by two highwaymen in 1776. Not all of the Spurrier family, of course, enjoyed great riches and comforts: Captain Christopher Spurrier, the half-pay captain of a naval ship, lived in a comparatively modest house in Market Street, as did John Spurrier, the sailmaker, in Strand Street.

Having gained power, as well as wealth in Poole and Newfoundland, it was natural that the thoughts of the head of the family should turn to a seat in Parliament for one of the Spurriers. By the early 1800's the Lesters, the Garlands and John Jeffery had shown how it was possible to win one of Poole's two seats in the Commons and, in 1807, William Spurrier thought the time ripe to secure the election of his son Christopher. George Garland, one of the sitting members had decided not to contest the next election and Christopher was groomed to succeed him. However, his father blundered badly, ruined his son's chances, and himself experienced the great displeasure of the House of Commons.

William Spurrier had calculated that if he could obtain and conceal the writ ordering the election in Poole, he would gain some advantage for his son. Accordingly, he took the writ from an attorney's office in London, pretending that he was merely going to deliver it to the Sheriff of Poole, and then concealed it for a fortnight. Inevitably his deception came to light and the Commons proceeded to investigate this breach of parliamentary privilege; the hapless old man, now pleading for clemency because he was "now of the age of 73 years and upwards, and is very lame, deaf and otherwise infirm," was detained by the Sergeant at Arms. Two days later he was escorted to the Bar of the House of Commons, rebuked for interfering with the writ "from motives of undue favour and partiality," and ordered to be discharged, although a minority of members wanted him to be kept in custody for a week longer to teach him a lesson.

This public disgrace must have been felt very greatly by William Spurrier for he had watched over the great rise in the fortunes of his firm and had been much respected in the trade and in the town: in Newfoundland, where he had worked for a long time, he had been appointed by the Government to be Naval officer for St Mary's, Oderin, Burin and Mortier Bay. He lived only two years after his disgrace and it fell to the young Christopher to take over control of the family's business, which by this time included a bank in Poole. To provide himself with assistance he took two partners: his nephew William Jubber Spurrier, who inherited half of the wealth of Thomas Jubber, a merchant from an old Poole family whose two sons had "died abroad", and Peter Jolliffe (1764-1832) who was his uncle.

However, his father's grave blunder did nothing to diminish Christopher Spurrier's political ambitions. For the moment, it is true, he had to stand by and see George Garland's son take the Poole seat he had hoped for, but he began to make sure of eventually being elected by coming to an understanding with George

Garland that he would help Christopher in a future election, if possible in Poole.

He had matrimonial ambitions as well, and here again the Garlands could help, for their eldest daughter Amy was probably the most eligible young woman in Poole at this time. As the Napoleonic Wars drew to a close, the young head of the great Spurrier commercial house enjoyed himself in fashionable resorts, now in Ryde, then in Weymouth, now in London and then in France, his thoughts filled with the fine house he planned to build outside Poole and how his marriage to Amy would help him to make a proper entry into county and London society. At this very time, too the foundation of his fortunes, the Newfoundland trade, echoed his happy thoughts as it enjoyed its last period of great prosperity: the ten ships the family then had registered in Poole and the numerous others which had been built in Newfoundland scurried across the Atlantic and into the Mediterranean to keep pace with the demand for cod in liberated Europe.

His marriage took place in 1814. George Garland did all that he could to make it successful for his cherished daughter, providing a dowry of £4,000 (with an additional £2,000 to be held until Christopher Spurrier should need it to fight an election) and even persuading the Archbishop of Canterbury to waive the normal rules of residence for Spurrier. Amy left her father with a present of £50 and advice "to study her husband and to be good to Mrs Spurrier and her mother." However, all of Garland's careful preparations could not check the impetuous Spurrier. He was determined to intervene in the next election to make himself member for Poole and in 1817 launched a bitter political quarrel with his father-in-law, who alleged with much justice that Spurrier had broken his word by insisting on coming forward as a candidate. This quarrel, carried on partly in public in the columns of the local newspaper, can hardly have helped Spurrier's marriage and despite George Garland's efforts to heal the breach, it was not until 1824 that a rather stiff reconciliation took place.

In the meantime Spurrier had at least realised one ambition in becoming MP for Bridport in 1820, with the aid of H C Sturt of More Crichel, while in 1824, with the help of his father-in-law, he was chosen as High Sheriff of Dorset. These achievements cost a great deal of money: the Bridport election forced him to raise a £12,000 mortgage on Upton House and to sell his Compton Abbas estate for £16,513. Public life meant too that he had even less time than before for the family business and, while other merchants, like George Garland, were beginning to reduce their commitments in the Newfoundland trade, sensing that the post war depression which came over it would not pass as easily as earlier periods of bad trade, Spurrier and his partners appear not to have altered course.

His marriage too was under strain; a daughter Amy had been born in 1815, a second baby daughter died in 1818 and a son was stillborn in 1821. Spurrier however appears to have continued down his primrose path and was to be found in most of the fashionable resorts of the day – Paris, Florence and even Mudeford! Yet the pace was beginning to tell on his finances and in 1828 he sold Upton House to Edward Doughty. Carefree to the end, he then gambled away his paintings and his

Ryde, Isle of Wight, in the 19th century.

Lisbon, one of the main centres for the import of fish from Newfoundland.
A 19th century view.

Sir,

In consequence of the failure of the firm of Messrs. C. SPURRIER and Co., whose extensive connections in Newfoundland, must necessarily delay the adjustment of the concerns of the Estate, and postpone the payment of a Dividend, if some plan is not adopted to give facility to the Creditors in that Country for proving their debts; we forward you herewith an Affidavit to prove your debts, and a Power of Attorney to authorise any friend whose name you may think proper to insert in it, to receive your Dividend, and also Instructions annexed for the due execution of them.

Upon your returning them completed, your Dividend will be paid to your Correspondent here as soon as they are ordered by the Commissioners. The amount of your Account as it stands in the Books of Messrs. C. SPURRIER and Co. here, is £

It is difficult in such cases to speak with accuracy as to the probable amount of Dividend, but the debts appear to amount to £26,077 16s.; and besides the amount to be realized for the Trade, the opinion of a most eminent Counsel has been obtained, who advises that the Life Estate of Mr. C. SPURRIER, in his Settlement money, £33,333, 3 per cent. Consols, belongs to the Creditors, the terms of the Settlement having given Mr. SPURRIER a life interest, but in the event of Bankruptcy or Insolvency, the Life Estate to be payable to the exclusive use of the Wife, which the law will not allow; the value of this is supposed to be £10,000, so that the Estate will, in all probability, pay a good Dividend: the separate Debts of the parties, we are told, are not much, and we are informed there will be a surplus from each of the separate Estates. As our client Mr. GEO. GARLAND, is one of the Assignees, we would suggest the propriety of your introducing the names of GEORGE GARLAND of the Town and County of Poole, Merchant, and JOHN BINGLEY GARLAND, of the same place, Merchant, as the parties to whom the power should be given.

We are, Sir,

Your most obedient Servants,

To

A letter from the Receivers in Bankruptcy about the disposal of Christopher Spurrier's estates.

silver. One family story of these days has been handed down to us and tells of a dinner party he gave. When Christopher and his guests reached their port and nuts it was found that the walnuts had maggots in them. Unabashed by the state of the walnuts he challenged his friends to a race between the maggots from their walnuts. They measured a suitable course and Christopher wagered his last silver tea pot on the race. Unfortunately his maggot turned out to be of a lazy disposition, probably having gorged itself rather too freely of his walnut, and so Spurrier, to encourage it forward, applied a pin to what he took to be the rear quarters of the maggot. However, far from achieving the desired result the prick promptly killed his maggot stone dead and he lost his tea pot!

Other calamities, in which he was not the only sufferer, brought the firm of Christopher Spurrier, Peter Jolliffe and William Jubber Spurrier to as sudden an end as that suffered by his costly maggot. There had been some revival in the Newfoundland trade in the 1820's but this had not prevented some of the Poole traders in twine, spirits and other items for Newfoundland from going bankrupt. In 1829 came ominious reports of a bad fishing season, followed by the shocking news in July 1830 that the leading house of Spurrier, Jolliffe and Spurrier had collapsed with over £26,000 in debts.

Some idea of the magnitude of this crash may be obtained from the schedule of properties which the Spurriers possessed. In Poole itself there was a mansion and counting house in West Street, other properties in the High Street, a coal and timber wharf on the West Shore, to say nothing of the fleet of eleven ocean going ships registered in Poole, the pride of which was a vessel of 320 tons, ironically called the "Upton" after the mansion Christopher had already sacrificed. (The *Upton* was the largest vessel, and possibly the only "ship" ever to be built in Newfoundland for it was the only one of the many vessels built there which is known to have had three masts.) All these properties went under the Auctioneer's hammer on 30 December 1830, but even they were hardly as impressive as the range of properties which now had to be sold up in Newfoundland. This involved large business premises in Placentia Bay at Burin, Oderin, Barren Island and the Isle of Allan. There was for example at Burin, the main centre of their business, a large house with eight bedrooms, no fewer than six stores, as well as offices, coopers' and carpenters' shops, drying "flakes" which could take 900 quintals (hundredweights) of fish, and even three batteries of guns to protect the station from attack.

Christopher Spurrier's brothers-in-law, George Garland (Junior) and John Bingley Garland, were appointed receivers in bankruptcy and had the unpleasant task of finding money to pay his creditors. Their task was made difficult by the depressed state of the Newfoundland trade and by the nature of the marriage settlement Christopher had arranged when he had married Amy Garland. The receivers naturally wished to preserve as much as possible of the sum involved for their unfortunate sister but the hapless Christopher had unwittingly made the settlement in such a way that it now had by law to be set aside and the money given over to help provide for the creditors. They were soon reassured that "the Estate will, in all probability, pay a good Dividend."

The winding up of the Spurrier empire in Newfoundland meant the final failure of all the strivings for success made not only by Christopher Spurrier's family but by all those Poole men who had built up the firms taken over by the Spurriers, and more recently the efforts of the Jubber family. However, the downfall of the Spurriers did not completely destroy the link between Poole and the south side of Newfoundland. John Hooper, a native of Poole, remained in business at Mortier, close to Burin, the Spurrier's old station. In 1833 he was elected member for Burin in the first Newfoundland legislative assembly. He also served as Naval officer at Burin, a position William Spurrier had filled years before. In Poole, the Corporation took an interest in the disposal of Spurrier's property because they wanted some of it in the High Street in order to widen the road. Having made arrangements to buy this "without the concurrence of the bankrupts themselves," (evidently an early 19th century version of a compulsory purchase order!) the Corporation proceeded to take over the premises. However, when it came to dispose of the property surplus to its road widening scheme no acceptable bids were received at the auction, for the decline of the Newfoundland trade meant that the property market in Poole was in the doldrums. The Corporation then decided to try to sell the premises by private treaty for £900. Months later no buyer had been found and the Corporation held a special meeting to appoint yet another committee to deal with their encumbrance. Despairingly they instructed this committee to fix a price for the building materials if no buyer could be found for the land and properties. Within a month however their search for a buyer ended and Robert Turtle, one of their members and a bootmaker, bought the property for £700, possibly for his son who was an accountant in the town.

Disposing of the Spurrier's property was not the only problem that the family's crash brought to the Corporation: late in 1829 Thomas Henry Spurrier, a young member of the family had been elected Water Bailiff, one of the junior offices in the Corporation which was the first step towards the exalted positions of Sheriff and Mayor. By 1831 Thomas Spurrier was, not surprisingly, no longer resident in the town and a special meeting of the Corporation had to be summoned solemnly to remove him from office. With this resolution the Corporation ended the civic career of a family which had played a leading role in its affairs since Timothy Spurrier's election to the Corporation one hundred and twelve years previously.

When the receivers had done their work Amy Spurrier was able to recover £5,000 from her husband's estate. She lived only ten years more, often apart from the wayward Christopher, despite the efforts of the Garland family to bring about a reconciliation.

As for Christopher Spurrier – he had lost his gamble for fame: his house, his riches, his public life and his marriage were gone. Yet he clung to life and did not die until 1876 at the ripe old age of 93, rather to the relief of his son-in-law, Baron de Linden of Wurtemburg who probably had to help support the long declining years

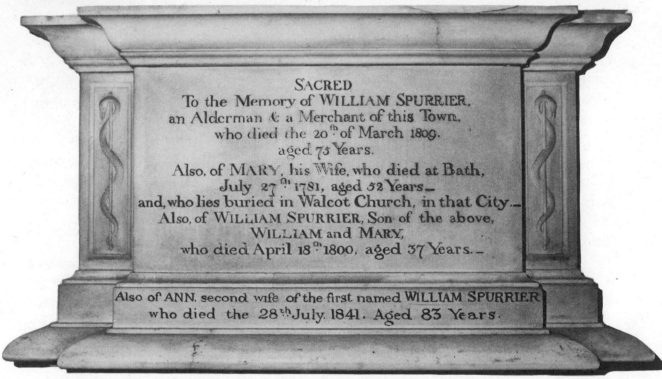

SACRED
To the Memory of WILLIAM SPURRIER,
an Alderman & a Merchant of this Town,
who died the 20th of March 1809.
aged 75 Years.

Also, of MARY, his Wife, who died at Bath,
July 27th 1781, aged 52 Years—
and, who lies buried in Walcot Church, in that City—
Also, of WILLIAM SPURRIER, Son of the above,
WILLIAM and MARY,
who died April 18th 1800, aged 37 Years.—

Also of ANN, second wife of the first named WILLIAM SPURRIER
who died the 28th July, 1841. Aged 83 Years.

The Spurrier Monument in St James's Church, Poole.

of the builder of Upton House and the last merchant princeling of the Spurrier line.

It is, however, very doubtful whether Christopher Spurrier had ever been thought of as the son to take on the Spurrier empire. His elder brother William had unfortunately died in 1800 at the age of 37 and Christopher, if he ever had been trained in the business, did not seem to pay sufficient regard to it or even think very much about it at all; it was not in his character to question whether the great prosperity of those earlier years would last or whether it was wise simultaneously to lay out a marriage settlement of £20,000 and a large sum for a fine house at Upton. Like all merchants engaged in the Newfoundland trade, Christopher Spurrier was naturally something of a gambler; the merchants had to take great risks with their capital, but even among his fellow merchants Christopher Spurrier had a particular reputation as a gambler. Unfortunately for Christopher Spurrier, the very time he had spent so lavishly on his marriage, his new mansion and the purchase of his large estates was the moment when the Newfoundland trade began its final decline. In the period 1815-1817 many of the traders went bankrupt and many of the fishermen and planters (as the proprietors of the small fishing boats in Newfoundland were called) lost all the money which they had deposited in what they thought were the safe hands of the merchants. The most destitute of the Irish, who had then recently emigrated to Newfoundland in great numbers, were shipped back to Ireland at the Government's expense and many hundreds of the other settlers were taken over to Halifax in Nova Scotia to start a fresh life. The trouble basically was that the demand for Newfoundland fish was greatly reduced soon after the end of the European wars.

This period of Christopher Spurrier's lavish expenditure in fact, turned out to be just the time when prudent conservation of capital would have had its reward. He and his firm managed to weather this storm with the other merchants who had been long established in Newfoundland but, apart from a good year in 1819, the price of fish then fell to prices some 50% lower than it had been even in the early 1800's and this deepening depression, with consequential problems in Newfoundland, began to spell the end of the great firm of Spurrier & Co.

It was in an effort to keep his empire solvent that Christopher Spurrier had sold Upton House and its estates in 1828 and, from that year, it was the turn of the Tichborne family with its own brand of troubles to come to live in the mansion. At first, however, all was plain sailing for them. There was even an aura of the fairy tale in the way Edward Doughty came to own and occupy Upton House. Edward Doughty had been born Edward Tichborne, and was the third son of Baron Tichborne of Tichborne Park, one of the oldest Hampshire families and one of the richest. Edward like his younger brother James Tichborne, the fourth son, was given an allowance of £500 a year by the Baron. Edward's younger brother managed to live desultorily on his allowance and in 1827 had married a wife who, although half-English, had been brought up in France and had every intention of continuing to live in Paris. Edward himself, on the other hand, had taken a job on the Duke of Buckingham's sugar plantations in Jamaica until, in 1826, to the astonishment of the whole family, he was left the wealth and estates of a fourth cousin of the Tichborne's called Elizabeth Doughty. These estates included many valuable London properties round Gray's Inn as well as country estates, one of which was in Dorest near to Upton House.

Elizabeth Doughty had bequeathed her fortune to the third son of Baron Tichborne for the express purpose of starting a new family line of 'Doughty's' distinct from the Tichbornes. It was necessary for Edward Tichborne to change his name to Doughty to comply with the condition of his inheritance and, to start a new county family he had, of course, to have an appropriate house and estates. With part of his new fortune, therefore, Edward Tichborne, under his newly acquired name of Edward Doughty, bought Upton House and grounds from Christopher Spurrier. He then spent a little more of his fortune on a few extensions of the house including a chapel at one end of the building and, in 1828 when he was 46 years old, went to live there with his wife.

While Christopher Spurrier and his partners were vainly struggling to keep their firm solvent, the new Mr and Mrs Edward Doughty were busy engaging a large staff to run their new mansion and estate and happily preparing for a quiet life there. Perhaps the only person to be appointed to the household or to look after the gardens and estate at Upton who was not from the locality was a negro called Andrew Bogle, whom Edward had brought back from Jamaica. But even Andrew Bogle soon attained local affiliations by marrying a Poole girl, Miss Young, who was working at Upton House as nurse with Mrs Doughty.

Edward Doughty was never very well known in Poole. It was said that he was an "amiable and excellent gentleman", but he was deaf as well as having "an affliction of the nerves." This led him to keep generally aloof from public affairs – quite the reverse of Poole's other notable neighbour, Mr William Ponsonby (later Lord de Mauley) who had completed the rebuilding of Canford House to the north of Poole about the same time as the Doughtys had gone to Upton House.

Edward and Katherine Doughty's only substantial involvement in the affairs of Poole came from their families' position in the Catholic religion. Both the Tichbornes and the Seymour family, from which Katherine Doughty had come, were among the leading Catholic families in England. They were devout Catholics themselves and gave considerable help in the building of the first permanent Catholic church in Poole. In fact it was said in Poole at the time that the West Quay Road site was chosen because Mrs Doughty could then see the church from her drawing room at Upton House.

Otherwise Edward Doughty's afflictions seem to have kept him away from Poole, though he was seen at the town's regatta in 1830 with the Roman Catholic Bishop of London. In the same year, too, he was one of the local gentlemen who bade farewell to the exiled French King Charles X when he left Hamworthy for Scotland after his stay at Lulworth Castle. (Doughty had earlier lent his carriage to the King on his arrival in Poole, so that the fallen monarch could travel from Hamworthy to Lulworth in at least some style).

For a number of years thereafter Edward and Katherine Doughty lived the quiet life of the landed gentry at Upton House. Their son had died as a child and their only surviving child, Katherine, was born at Upton in 1834 and the news of the life and activity of the occupants and visitors, came from the retainers as they went to and from their work at Upton House and its estates.

Meanwhile, James Tichborne, Edward Doughty's brother living in Paris, had finally persuaded his wife to agree that their son Roger Tichborne could have an English education, and he was sent as a boarder to Stoneyhurst.

With his parents continuing to live in Paris it therefore became the habit of Roger Tichborne to spend his long school holidays with his uncle and aunt at Upton House. He was a few years older than his cousin Katherine but he came to know her very well as they grew up together, and both came to love Upton House and its grounds. At the end of his school days in 1848 it was again to Upton House that Roger came to study for the entrance examination for the Army. Almost to his own surprise Roger passed the Entrance Examination in 1849 and this slight, sallow looking young man of 20 joined the 6th Dragoon Guards, the Carabineers, and was stationed at Cahir near Waterford in Ireland for the next three years.

But as the Doughtys lived peacefully at Upton House, the vicissitudes of births and deaths were conspiring to defeat Elizabeth Doughty's plans to instigate a separate lineage of Doughtys.

In 1821, while Edward Doughty had been in Jamaica, and some five years before he had inherited Elizabeth Doughty's fortune, Henry Tichborne, his eldest brother, had inherited the Tichborne title and estates and, though his wife had a child at least every other year and finally ended with seven children, they were all girls and therefore could not inherit. Henry's brother, Benjamin, the next in line, had died earlier, so that Edward Doughty, the younger brother living at Upton had become heir apparent to the Tichborne titles and estates as soon as it became obvious that Henry was not going to have a son. Therefore when Edward did eventually inherit the Tichborne title, the Doughty fortune would again be combined with the Tichborne's and there would be no separate Doughty lineage after all.

Even Edward Doughty's likely inheritance of the Tichborne titles did not end the complications of inheritance, for Katherine Doughty was *his* only surviving child. Thus it would be his younger brother James, living in Paris with his rather neurotic wife, and their elder son, Roger Tichborne, who would inherit both fortunes on Edward's own death.

These facts seemed to spell the inevitable end of the Tichbornes at Upton House, for Edward Doughty duly became the 9th Baron Tichborne in 1845 on his brother's death and, though he was in no hurry to move from Upton House to the ancestral home of the Tichborne's at Alresford, it was inevitable that he would have to move there sooner or later.

Such a move would mean, of course, that there was little need for the family, now united as Tichbornes again, to have a second family house and estate. The sale of Upton House therefore seemed the next logical step, especially as the Tichborne

Sir Edward Doughty

Lady Doughty

Alfred Tichborne, brother of Sir Roger.

Sir James Tichborne

estates had been heavily mortaged to provide the dowries for the previous Baron's seven daughters. However, the formal combination of the larger Doughty fortunes with those of the Tichborne's, and the sale of the Upton House and estates, needed the signature of his nephew, Roger Tichborne, as the next in line. Edward Doughty, now the 9th Baron Tichborne but still at Upton, and his younger brother James immediately agreed that this should be done as soon as Roger Tichborne came of age in 1850.

When the matter had been broached to Roger Tichborne earlier he had not seemed well disposed to such an arrangement and when his father and uncle redoubled their efforts to persuade him to enter into such a Deed after he had come of age it led to quarrels between the three men.

The ensuing arguments between Roger Tichborne and his uncle and father were the root cause of the many tribulations which beset the family, and led to Upton House and its owners becoming the talking point of the world some years later. What Roger Tichborne possibly did not tell his father and uncle at the time, was that he had fallen in love with his cousin Katherine and she with him – and both of them with Upton House. Roger therefore had not the slightest intention of agreeing to sell Upton House, which he and "Katty" both loved, whatever his father and uncle did or said.

On the other hand, when Roger did confess his love for his cousin, it was his uncle and aunt's turn to be equally obdurate. Lady Tichborne, as Mrs Katherine Doughty then was, thought little of Roger Tichborne as the husband of her daughter. She, as a devoted Catholic, thought Roger was too nearly related in blood to Katherine. Moreover she considered Roger to be irreligious; he "drowns thought of the future in drink, and offends Almighty God by profane language," she said. Finally, despite sporadic efforts by Roger to mend his ways, things got so bad between the members of the Tichborne family that Sir Edward in 1852 forbade his nephew to see his daughter ever again and banned him from Tichborne Park.

The quarrels ended with Roger, who had in any case always wished to travel, deciding to leave the country altogether. He resigned his commission in the Army and, using Upton House as his base, prepared to sail to South America, saying that if Katherine was not engaged to be married by the end of 1854 he would return to marry her.

With one personal servant, John Moore, the son of his butler at Upton House, he sailed from Le Havre in a French sailing vessel in March 1853. Twelve days later the ship had got as far as Falmouth and, a further ninety-nine days later, it finally arrived at Valparaiso. Roger stayed in South America for the rest of the year visiting Chile and other South American countries but for the most part living a rather dissolute life and, in the process, quarrelled with his companion, John Moore, whom he dismissed early in his stay in Valparaiso.

The next year he sailed on his own from Rio de Janeiro on a ship called "The Bella" for New York—and that was the last that was ever heard of such a ship.

Nothing was heard of Roger Tichborne either, and in due course he was presumed drowned at sea.

His uncle Edward, the 9th Baron, had died in 1853 while Roger was still in South America and his father had become the 10th Baron Tichborne. By this time no one had any doubts that Roger had perished at sea, that is, except his mother, Henriette, who had never accepted that her elder son was dead. She frequently told of the presentiments she had that she would see him again. She was now Lady Tichborne of course, and as such had to live mainly at Tichborne Park and there for the following 9 years she waited for news of her son Roger, avidly listening to any stories from returned sailors which bolstered her hopes of seeing Roger again.

However nothing had been heard of Roger before her husband died in 1862, and her younger son Alfred succeeded to the title as the 11th Baron Tichborne. This son was eccentric and outrageously reckless – so much so that within a year of succeeding to the title he was bankrupt! He borrowed £40,000 from an Insurance Company on the security of his life interest in the estates and, even then, succeeded in going bankrupt again, and even managed to get himself imprisoned for a time at Winchester.

Lady Tichborne now became even more frantic to find her elder son Roger. She advertised for news of him. Sympathetic clairvoyants promised she would see her son again within three years, and the rest of the story of Upton House and the Tichbornes lies enshrined in the reports of the two most famous cases in British legal history, generally known as the Tichborne cases.

The process started with an Inquiry Agent in Australia seeing Lady Tichborne's advertisement. There were then many missing people in Australia. Many black sheep of Victorian families ended in Australia. Those times, too, saw the Australian gold-rush and, of course, criminals had been regularly transported there as punishment between 1790 and 1850. It was therefore commonplace for men to change their names, or even to have a selection of names in Australia.

It was, too, not surprising that this Agent at Gippsland Australia, trying to collect a small debt from a butcher there who called himself Castro, began to wonder whether this man, who said he had big assets in England, was not the missing Roger Tichborne. The Agent decided, after some questioning of the butcher Castro, that he was indeed Roger Tichborne. According to this Agent, Castro was "hugely disgusted" at being found out, but finally agreed to write to Lady Tichborne. His letter of 1866 started by saying "The delay which has taken place since my last letter dated 22 April '54 makes it very difficult . . ." and it was probably no exaggeration!

Lady Tichborne was herself at first suspicious and did not respond immediately. She consulted her solicitors who restrained her further, and it was only when she had received photographs from Australia, some nine months later, that she committed herself as far as to send the passage money to the Claimant – the name by which the world was shortly to know the man who, calling himself Castro and earlier as Orton, claimed that he really was Roger Tichborne. But by the time the money from Lady Tichborne was received in Australia, the Claimant had in fact already borrowed enough to book a passage for himself and family to come to England.

Even before the Claimant had sailed, his claim to the Tichborne title and estates was news in the Press both in Australia and Britain. To make his way to England he had to go to Sydney to board a ship and, by coincidence, Andrew Bogle the negro servant who had returned with Edward Tichborne from Jamaica, was then living in Sydney. (On the death of her husband Lady Tichborne, the previous Mrs Doughty, had pensioned off Andrew Bogle and he had then emigrated with his family to Australia.) Andrew Bogle on seeing the news that the man claiming to be Roger Tichborne was in Sydney, went round to his hotel to meet him, for Bogle had had much to do with Roger at Upton House and at Tichborne Park.

When Bogle arrived at the hotel he found that the Claimant was out so he sat down in the courtyard of the hotel to await the Claimant's return. As the Claimant returned he saw Bogle and shouted to him, "Bogle, is that you?" and, seeing some surprise on Bogle's face, added "Yes, Bogle, I am not the slender lad I was at Tichborne!" and, from that encounter, the Claimant had immediately recruited one of his strongest and most consistent supporters in his claim to the Baronetcy of Tichborne. He soon persuaded Andrew Bogle to return to England.

The Claimant finally arrived in England on Christmas Day 1866. His mother was not at her London house; she had gone to Paris. The Claimant booked into a London hotel and visited Alresford and Tichborne Park and met many of the local people who had known Roger Tichborne. Most of them were happy to accept him as "Sir Roger" and the Tichborne family solicitor was willing to act for him. For some reason the Claimant refused this offer and appointed a young solicitor called Holmes on a casual recommendation made to him in a London public house. The Claimant in his stay in London also made a couple of visits to Wapping to make enquiries of the family of Orton, visits which were later to give him much trouble in explaining.

However, having got himself a solicitor, the Claimant borrowed his first £20 in England from the solicitor to transport himself to Paris to meet Lady Tichborne. He and his claim were already such news that there was a crowd at London Bridge station to see him off on his journey and, from that day the Claimant was hardly out of the news for years to come.

By this time the Claimant was hardly the rather tall man of 'delicate constitution', as Lady Tichborne had described him in her advertisements. He was over 13 stones in weight when he finally presented himself to Lady Tichborne in Paris. Nevertheless, Lady Tichborne was utterly convinced that he was indeed her son Roger. The Claimant's solicitor immediately wrote to The Times telling the world that Lady Tichborne had recognised her son and that they were returning to England to take up his inheritance. This brought a quick reply from the Tichborne solicitor, though none of the other Tichbornes had so much as seen him. They wrote "Our instructions are to deny emphatically that your client is the person he represents himself to

Andrew Bogle, who it is thought returned to Poole and was buried in Hamworthy Churchyard.

Mr Alfred Seymour who became the Claimant's chief adversary after Henry Danby Seymour's withdrawal from the battle. He was MP for Salisbury.

be, and to leave him to adopt such measures as he thinks proper." The disputed Tichborne inheritance was now really a *cause celebre*.

It was now obvious that the Claimant, despite Lady Tichborne's certain recognition of him as her son, was not going to be accepted by the Tichborne family without a fight. The Claimant and his solicitor therefore set about getting as many affidavits as possible from people willing to swear that the Claimant was Roger Tichborne. Their first call was to Alresford where the family solicitor, the family doctor and other locally well-known people all accepted the Claimant as Roger Tichborne. At first it must have seemed they had a relatively easy task ahead of them.

There was, however, one very notable exception to this recognition and this was Henry Danby Seymour, the Member of Parliament for Poole who, with his brother, was the fiercest and most implacable opponent of the Claimant. H Danby Seymour had won the seat for the Whig (or Liberal) interest in the by-election of 1850 caused by the death of G R Robinson, a "Liberal Conservative" who had been a particularly suitable Member for Poole in that he had been the Chairman of Lloyds and had had close connections with the Newfoundland trade as a partner in the London firm of Robinson, Brooking & Garland.

What, however, was more pertinent to the story of the Claimant and Upton House was that Henry Danby Seymour MP was the brother of Lady Tichborne. There was nothing his half-sister could ever do which pleased Henry Seymour and, even before Lady Tichborne had so much as seen the Claimant, he had pleaded with her on no account to recognise him as her son. When she did do so, he felt it was as his bounden duty to the family to rectify the harm she had done by all the means in his power.

For a long time Henry Seymour refused to meet the Claimant at all. He had been convinced from the beginning that the Claimant was a fraud and to him, therefore, anything was fair that would show up the Claimant for the imposter he was.

In October 1867, for instance, Henry Seymour MP was on one of his most infrequent visits to his constituency, staying at the London Hotel in High Street, when he was told that the Claimant was arriving by train at Poole that afternoon. On hearing this Mr Seymour approached a local man, William Gould, who was known to have gone on many fishing and hunting expeditions with Roger Tichborne when he was living at Upton House. Henry Seymour asked Mr Gould to meet the train so that he could have a good look at the Claimant and could then return to Henry Seymour to confirm that the Claimant was not Roger Tichborne.

Mr Gould agreed to do this but, when he saw the Claimant step off the train, had "instantly recognised" him as Roger Tichborne. According to the affidavit subsequently sworn by William Gould "in the evening of the same day I again saw Mr H D Seymour, and in answer to his questions I told him that I had seen the gentleman and was sure he was the same person as the Mr Roger Tichborne I formerly knew, and there was no mistake about it, and I would swear to him anywhere. The said Mr Seymour was much annoyed at my communication, and left me directly." Seymour, to avoid the Claimant who had come to stay at the same hotel, immediately packed his belongings and hurriedly left Poole never to return at least while he was its Member of Parliament.

However, Henry Seymour did eventually meet the Claimant. Some time later he arranged to see the Claimant in London and he took with him Mr Burden of Poole, who had been the butler at Upton House. Mr Seymour, however, had got Mr Burden to dress up as a gentleman of fashion of those days and was delighted by his stratagem for, when he asked the Claimant if he recognised his companion, the Claimant took the fashionably-dressed Mr Burden to be one of his uncles!

Mr Burden was from that day the Claimant's only Poole adversary. Poole people were almost to a man believers in the Claimant's cause. Police Constable No 4 of the Poole Police, for instance, who had formerly worked in the Upton House stables, said he immediately recognised the Claimant as being Roger Tichborne as he got out of the omnibus at the London Hotel. He had told his Sergeant and Superintendent, and had again identified the Claimant later in their presence. Mr Crabb, an Upton House gardener, was equally certain of the Claimant's identity. Charles Adams of Upton, many years a labourer on Sir Edward Doughty's estate, had no doubts. Mrs Hussey who had been in service at Upton House when Roger Tichborne had visited the house swore that she "perfectly well remembers him and is perfectly sure that he is the same person." Mr Robert Bromby, a Customs Officer, remembered "chasing a goose with him," and Robert Cherrett of Lytchett, who had made packing cases for Roger Tichborne to take to South America had "no hesitation in desposing to his identity."

What, perhaps, was more surprising, in view of the Claimant's growing size, was that William Clench, tailor in High Street, Poole, swore that he had measured and made clothes for Roger Tichborne before he went to South America, that the Claimant was this same person. Martha Legg, the laundress at Upton House was convinced that the Claimant was Roger Tichborne for other reasons. She knew he must have been Roger Tichborne because he reminded her that the shirts she had so often laundered for him at Upton House had stags' heads embroidered on them and his handkerchiefs were adorned with bulls' and dogs' heads. This was when after his return she had first seen him in the Lion Hotel at Poole: she had gone over to him and said straight away "How do you do, Sir Roger?" and he had then talked of his shirts' embroidery. "No other person could have said to me what Sir Roger said when I went into the room", she averred. There was, too, the most faithful Andrew Bogle who had returned from Australia with the Claimant – and whose honourable part in the cases was in great contrast to the conduct of many of the others involved.

The Claimant's solicitor was progressing his case well: his client had been recognised by his mother, his lawyer, his doctor, his Army servants and many people from Upton House. His old sweetheart Katherine Doughty, who had married while Roger Tichborne had been in South America and was then Mrs Radcliffe, at first recognised him as Roger, but was less sure than some. She said that she recognised her cousin "by his eyes, eyebrows and shape of his forehead"

POOLE ELECTION.

At a Meeting of the Electors of the TOWN and County and Borough of POOLE, held at the *GUILDHALL*,

this 23rd day of September, 1850, for Electing One Burgess to Serve for the said Town and County and Borough in the present Parliament, which was Summoned to be holden at the City of Westminster, the 21st day of September, 1847, and from thence prorogued to and until the 18th day of November then next ensuing, on which last named day the said Parliament was begun and holden, and from thence by several adjournments and prorogrations to and until the 15th day of October, now next following, stands adjourned and prorogued.

JOHN SAVAGE, Esq. was proposed by GEORGE LEDGARD, Esq., and Seconded by JAMES SLADE, Esq., as a fit and proper Person to Represent this Town and County and Borough in Parliament.

HENRY DANBY SEYMOUR, Esq., was proposed by GEORGE LOCKYER PARROTT, Esq., and Seconded by GEORGE PENNEY, Esq., as a fit and proper Person to Represent this Town and County and Borough in Parliament.

THE SHOW OF HANDS of the ELECTORS at such Meeting being in favor of

HENRY DANBY SEYMOUR, Esq.,

And a Poll being demanded on behalf of the said JOHN SAVAGE, Esquire, *I DO HEREBY GIVE NOTICE*, that such Poll will be taken To-morrow the 24th instant, and will commence at the hour of EIGHT of the Clock in the forenoon,' at the Polling Places or Booths in the said Borough, appointed by me for that purpose, and close precisely at FOUR o'Clock in the Afternoon.

DATED this 23rd day of September, 1850.

HENRY HARRIS, JUN.,
SHERIFF.

LANKESTER. PRINTER, HIGH STREET, POOLE.

and that she could not be sure that the Claimant was not Roger. However, before the trial started she had hardened to the thought that the Claimant could not really be Roger because he did not know many of the things which she considered he ought to have remembered.

From the time he first landed at London docks till his death the Claimant was always in deep financial trouble. From the start, when he had borrowed the money for his passage to England, he was a drain on the finances of everybody with whom he came into contact, his "mother", his friends, his supporters, his bankers, the public, even his lawyers and the moneylenders themselves (to whom he was finally promising to pay 50% interest and more). "Had I known it before I left Australia, I would never have wrote or come home to have caused such trouble and to have been such a drag on your purse," he wrote later to the dying Lady Tichborne. "I hope," he ended this letter, "to be able to repay you all back again and to see you happy and comfortable at Upton . . . I will send you a couple of photographs of Upton, the north and south front."

The legal battles started with the examination in Chancery of the case based on the affidavits which the Claimant and his solicitor had obtained. At this examination the Claimant said that he had given the agent of the Tichborne estates a sealed package (to be opened in case of his death) which instructed the agent not to sell Upton House and estates, to show great kindness to his cousin Kate and to let her live at Upton House if she so wished. The Claimant also told the Court, quite gratuitously and quite irrelevantly as far as his own case was concerned, that he had, in fact, secretly married Katherine Doughty after seducing her, and that at the time he was preparing to go to South America she had been very worried because she thought she was pregnant.

Such evidence would be of considerable news value today, but in 1867, such a "blasting of the reputation" of his cousin, who was now Lady Radcliffe, was an accusation which outraged polite society even as far as Queen Victoria herself. It added even greater heat to the quarrel and served finally to cement together the various strands of the Tichborne family into an implacable opposition to the Claimant. Moreover it eventually was to add seven years to the Claimant's incarceration.

The Tichborne lawyers obviously were not going to accept any of the Claimant's evidence as to his travels in South America, his story of his ordeal by shipwreck and the delirium he suffered as a result. These stories all too readily explained any lack of detail he was able to give of his life before his arrival in England. There were too, long periods of his stay in Australia unexplained. On the other hand, the cost of bringing to court all the witnesses, scattered round the world in South America, Australia and France, to the Court was a daunting expense even to the Tichborne purse. The Court therefore agreed to the appointment of a Commission to go out to these places in the first instance to take evidence so that it could be first decided which of the many potential witnesses should be called, and this decision inevitably meant a very great delay before the Claimant's case could come before the Court.

" . . . I will send you a couple of photographs of Upton, the north and the south front."

Upton House, 1876

It is difficult to conceive how the Claimant, his solicitor and the dowager Lady Tichborne considered they could have financed the case previously. The Court's decision to send a Commission first to South America and then to Australia and Tasmania must have made their position seem impossible. Lady Tichborne had herself little money to spare after making the Claimant an allowance of £1,000 a year. He, for his part, was not even managing on this allowance, for he was living as if he were Baron Tichborne already. Moreover, with his rich living, his weight was increasing alarmingly. It seemed that the more his creditors pressed him for their money the greater his weight became until, in a curious way, his two greatest concerns met in a simple equation when the Claimant's ever-increasing girth would no longer be accommodated in his trousers and Mr Poole, his tailor, refused to let them out yet again until he had been paid for his trousers' previous enlargement!

Then, in 1868, as they waited for the appointment of the Commission, the Claimant suffered a series of most serious setbacks. In March the dowager Lady Tichborne suddenly died. His "mother's" certain recognition of him was the cardinal point in the Claimant's case. Her death was so unexpected that the Claimant immediately thought of Henry Danby Seymour and suspected the worst possible cause for her death. He rushed round to Howlett's Hotel where Lady Tichborne had died and there met Henry Seymour, who had himself gone to the hotel on hearing the news. In the fierce quarrel which ensued the Claimant called Henry Seymour a "bloody blackguard", and it ended with the Claimant asserting his position as next-of-kin to demand that there should be an inquest to determine how Lady Tichborne had died.

The subsequent inquest determined that Lady Tichborne had died of natural causes, but this decision did nothing to assuage the hatred which had now risen between the Claimant and the Tichborne family. The hatred was even further heightened at Lady Tichborne's ensuing funeral when the Claimant, much to the indignation of the Tichbornes, asserted his right to the position as her chief mourner.

The quarrel which then ensued led a pro-Claimant Poole newspaper to lament "the unseemly contest which took place over her corpse, between the son of the departed Lady and Mr Alfred Seymour, the member for Totnes." "It is simply shocking" said the Poole Pilot, "that they should select her burial place as the scene of their disputes; that a brother of the departed Lady should try to displace from the position of chief mourner the individual whom his sister acknowledged as her son."

By the time of Lady Tichborne's funeral Henry Seymour was abroad. He himself was in deep financial trouble, not from spending his own money to defeat the Claimant but from the result of the crash of the Imperial Mercantile Financial Co for which he owed £24,000 in past "calls" on his shares with a further £16,000 then shortly due in further calls to be made upon them. As the local Poole paper succinctly put it: "To avoid difficulties arising out of these calls, Mr Seymour went abroad." He also resigned his seat in Parliament, now Poole's only seat, for the Reform Act of 1867 had reduced Poole's representation from two to one.

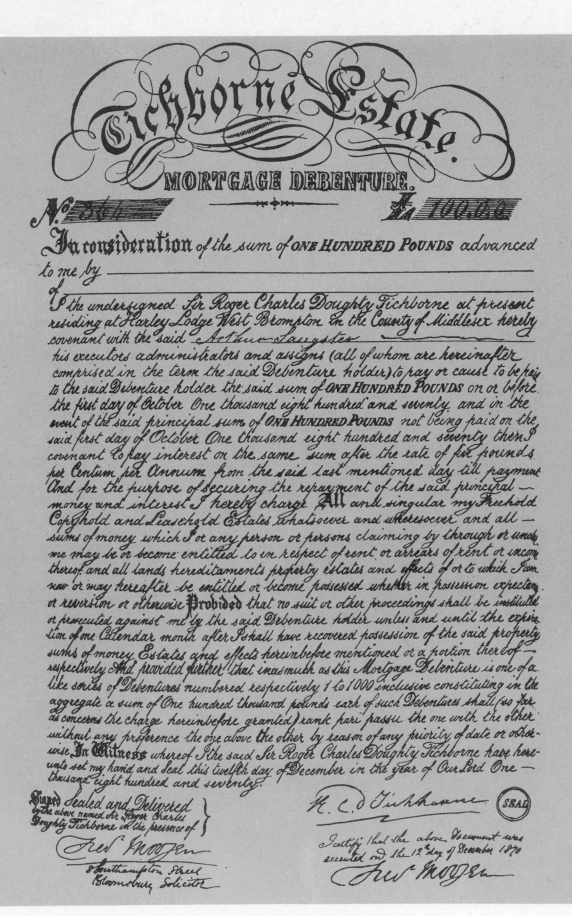

A 'Tichborne Bond'

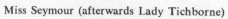
Miss Seymour (afterwards Lady Tichborne)

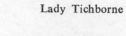
Lady Tichborne

Miss Kate Doughty at Upton

Mrs Seymour, wife of Henry Seymour.

40

However, the Commission appointed by the Court at last sailed off to South America. The Claimant and his solicitor's chief clerk accompanied them but, at Buenos Ayres the Claimant sailed no further. He said that he feared the sea trip round the Horn to go to Chile and would rather go overland. Then a little later, he changed his mind and took the first ship back to England, leaving the solicitor's clerk as the only one responsible for his interests in the interviews with potential witnesses and faced by the carefully appointed lawyers of the Tichborne family estate.

The gentry of Hampshire on the death of Lady Tichborne had agreed to support the Claimant to the sum of £1,400 a year but, on the premature return of the Claimant insisted on seeing him and did not accept his explanation that he had been ill in South America and in no condition to make the hazardous journey over the Andes to Chile. Many of them withdrew their financial backing.

The Claimant's luck seemed to be running out. The Tichborne family solicitor who had supported his identity died. Alfred Seymour pestered the Claimant's solicitor with anonymous, threatening letters. The creditors could be staved off no longer and the Claimant could borrow no more: he was made bankrupt. He then owed over £5,700 to his solicitor who was spending nearly the whole of his time on the case and getting little or no help from the Claimant who seemed to have become quite bored by the whole business. The solicitor had had enough. He, too, deserted the Claimant.

The new solicitor appointed by the now bankrupt Claimant had only one asset on which to pin any hope of raising the necessary money to advance his client's case, and that was the enormous public support which he had throughout the country, and this despite a generally hostile Press. The new solicitor's way of cashing in on this public support was to sell "Tichborne Bonds". These were "bonds" by which the Claimant promised the holder to pay him the face value of the bond within a month of getting possession of his Tichborne and Doughty estates. The bonds were sold at considerably less than their nominal value and found a ready market. So much so that £40,000 had soon been raised and the Claimant was put into the best financial position he had ever been in. He was again in a position to prosecute his claim.

The Commission had finally returned from its visits to South America and Australia where, with the Claimant's interests not fully represented, the witnesses chosen and the evidence obtained mainly favoured the Tichborne opposition. It had started, for instance, in Tasmania in May, 1869, and ended in Melbourne at the end of November. In this period it had interviewed 85 witnesses for the family and 29 for the Claimant and the questions of the Commission were often about events then 17 years previously.

However, the Claimant was at last able to brief Counsel and the case was set down for hearing in the Michaelmas list of 1870. But even then events seemed to have conspired to avoid a decision being reached for, at the date set down for hearing, all the first witnesses in the case, those who had known Roger in his youth in Paris, were under siege in Paris by the Germans in the Franco-Prussian war! So, in fact, the trial was not able to start until May 1871, over five years after the Claimant had first landed in Tilbury to claim the inheritance!

The trial had the maximum publicity and press coverage. Each day's proceedings seemed to raise some startling disclosure to keep it in the forefront of all the news of the day. To the harassed Lord Chief Justice, Sir William Bovill, it seemed that everybody in Britain wanted to attend the trial, and he, in turn, pestered the Government unceasingly to find larger premises to relieve the strain of the demands made on him. He had, in fact, on at least one occasion to find room for the Prince and Princess of Wales to come and witness the drama.

There was a sensation on the very first day of the trial. The enormous Press coverage leading up to the trial told vividly of the complications of the case, the involved emotions of the participants and the length of time the trial might take. This had so frightened those called for Jury Service that most of them disobeyed the Sheriff's summonses, stayed away from the Court, and it was thus impossible to empanel a Jury. This meant that the first day's trial had to be abandoned.

The furious Lord Chief Justice uttered dire threats of what would happen to the men summoned for Jury Service if they did not attend on the following day – again duly emblazoned in the Press. But even this only motivated nine of those summoned to attend the Court when it re-assembled on the following day. We do not know what happened to the recalcitrant jurors, but on the second day the frustrated Judges decided to proceed with the case with a Jury of only nine men.

The Claimant had no less than a hundred witnesses willing to swear on oath to the Court that he was indeed Roger Tichborne, the missing heir, but the world had to wait for many days till he himself was called to give evidence. A great deal depended on how the Claimant would fare under cross-examination by the eminent Counsel briefed by the Tichborne estate, and Serjeant Ballatine, the Claimant's Counsel, seemed reluctant to put the Claimant forward. The Claimant's cross-examination by Sir Henry Hawkins on behalf of the family would be the crucial battle, and everyone knew it.

The Claimant when his Counsel did finally put him in the witness box was asked over 35,000 questions. He did extremely well for himself at times. At other times he floundered on simple questions which many readers of the newspapers could have answered better. However, finally it was all over and, surprisingly, neither side could feel it had won. The Claimant's supporters argued that he had answered all but a few hundred questions correctly. The others were not too sure.

The Court adjourned before the Claimant's case had been finally put and, in the discussions in the Inns of Courts in the long Christmas recess, it was said that professional legal opinion was divided as to which side was winning.

The Claimant had done pretty well in court, but it was quite a different story as far as his finances were concerned. When the court broke up for the recess in November the Claimant had spent the whole of the £40,000 which had been raised

The Claimant

WILLIAM GOULD, FISHERMAN, OF POOLE.

Poole, March 14th, 1875.

DEAR SIR,—I have written these few lines to tell you that my poor wife died last Sunday of a broken heart. She was always crying about poor Sir ROGER TICHBORNE. Let her wake at what hour she might in the night, she was talking about him, and crying for putting an innocent man in prison. There is not one of his relations but know that it is Sir ROGER TICHBORNE that is in Dartmoor prison. Mr. ONSLOW, when will you want the Petitions, for I have got twenty sheets full at Poole? Please let me know when they will be wanted.—Yours,

WILLIAM GOULD, Fisherman.

To GUILDFORD ONSLOW, Esq.

Poole, April 26th,

DEAR SIR,—I have sent you my likeness, with Poole Harbour in the background. You must mind and tell the printer that when

ROGER TICHBORNE was in the boat with me,—fishing,—he always wore a net frock ; and be sure to tell the printer to have his frock and shirt-sleeves turned up above his elbows ; for when ROGER TICHBORNE and I used to pull the net into the boat, the first thing ROGER did was to pull off his coat, and turn up his shirt-sleeves above his elbows ; and if he had been tattooed, as Lord BELLEW swore, I must have seen the tattoo marks ; but I will swear before my God and Maker that ROGER TICHBORNE was not tattooed in the year 1852.

Sir, I have sent the model of the boat which Sir ROGER bought at Poole in the year 1852. And I should like to have both of us put into the boat, and please let Sir ROGER's shirt-sleeves be turned up above his elbows. No tattoo !!!

Mr. GRAY.

W. GOULD.

WILLIAM GOULD AND SIR ROGER TICHBORNE AT POOLE—NO TATTOO.

To the Editor of the ENGLISHMAN.

WILLIAM GOULD wishes these few lines to be inserted in the ENGLISHMAN about Sir ROGER TICHBORNE. "For the three months that he was staying at Upton House—October, November, December, in the year 1852—I was with him day and night. Sir ROGER TICHBORNE and myself have been fishing in the boat together. Both of us have stood up in a boat's stern, three feet wide, pulling the net over the stern of the boat ; and I have seen ROGER TICHBORNE pulling his shirt-sleeves above his elbows times out of number ; and *I have seen his naked arms scores of times, and will swear before my God and Maker that ROGER TICHBORNE NEVER was tattooed.* I have seen in the newspaper that Lady DORMER swore that she saw GOULD rowing ROGER TICHBORNE about in a boat at Upton, in the year 1848, but I will swear that I never spoke to ROGER TICHBORNE before the year 1852, and I know ROGER TICHBORNE as well as any man in England, for I was with him most of the time he was staying at Upton, the three months ; and the man that is suffering in Millbank Prison is no other man than Sir ROGER TICHBORNE.—Yours,

WILLIAM GOULD, Fisherman.

"Poole, Dorset.

"P.S.—I will go before all the magistrates in the world and swear that ROGER TICHBORNE was not tattooed in the year 1852."

by the Tichborne Bonds. When the court resumed its hearing in January, Serjeant Ballantine, the Claimant's leading Counsel was not being paid and, though still in charge of the case, often did not attend the court at all, and left matters to one or other of his juniors (the Claimant had briefed five Counsel and the family six). The Claimant himself seemed to become bored with the whole proceedings and more and more frequently did not bother to attend the court which the rest of the world was clamouring to get into.

However, on the 103rd day of the trial Serjeant Ballantine happened to be in court when some Defence witnesses first asserted that the real Roger Tichborne had certain tattoo marks on his arm – which the Claimant clearly had not got. The Jury were very impressed by this sudden evidence which they had not heard about before, any more than anybody else in court had, and they suddenly decided they had been convinced. They asked the Judges to stop the case. Rather than have that, Serjeant Ballantine on behalf of the Claimant said he would prefer the Court to 'non-suit' the Claimant. Then surprisingly, and without the matter having been put to the Claimant, or him being given any opportunity to give any contrary story, the Judges not only stopped the case but forthwith went on to issue a Writ of Perjury against the Claimant!

This calamitous end to the Claimant's case happened suddenly in Court with the Claimant not even being present. It must, therefore, have been a very surprised Claimant whom the Court bailiffs found in the Waterloo Hotel to be told that not only had he lost his case but he was being arrested for perjury on the Judge's Writ, and forthwith taken to Newgate Gaol. This was on 7 March 1872, ten months after the start of his case.

There was a great upsurge of public feeling in favour of the Claimant on the outcome of his case and his subsequent arrest. Despite the Grand Jury finding a true bill for his prosecution and the Press being almost unanimously against him, the general public still believed him to be Roger Tichborne and felt that it was the "Establishment" which had somehow killed his claim.

For all that, it took quite a long time for Horace Pitt-Rivers to get his release from prison on bail. However, the Claimant was eventually bailed and smuggled out of prison to avoid the crowds which had assembled to welcome him, but it was not long before he met his well-wishers. On arriving at Alresford he found there were 3,000 people there to welcome him with flags and bands and bunting and cries of "Glory to Sir Roger!" Festivities only culminated at midnight with a display of fireworks: the members of the newly formed Tichborne Defence Fund from Southampton who had attended the celebrations must have got home very late that night.

The Claimant spent his time on bail being feted all over the country. He started at Southampton where a brass band paraded him down the High Street. For the next two nights thousands of people came to Perkins & Sons Depository to listen to him and his supporters. Then he had a triumphant journey to most of the large towns of England and Scotland. Everywhere there were multitudes of cheering

Mr Justice Mellor (from a sketch by the Claimant)

Sir A E Cockburn, Lord Chief Justice of England.

Serjeant Ballantine

Dr Kenealy

supporters until, finally, in April 1873 the case of "Regina V Castro" was eventually called.

This Crown prosecution of the Claimant for perjury attracted even greater notoriety than the first one. It seemed that everybody clamoured to get one of the scarce tickets to attend this most intriguing trial. The opening sentences of the report of the trial which was published a year or so later commenced, "The eyes of the civilised world were turned with anxiety to the Court of Queen's Bench on the first day of the great Tichborne Trial. A man appeared there who had been the theme of a million tongues for more than six years past . . ."

The public's anticipation of a most sensational trial was well borne out in practice. It turned out to be probably the most famous trial in British legal history. It was certainly the longest case ever to be tried in Britain as well as the most expensive. It was also the most reported case, and, unfortunately for everybody's peace of mind thereafter, one of the worst defended cases. Lord Rivers who had done so much to help the Claimant did him no service at all in recommending to him the services of Dr Edward Kenealy QC who was appointed so late in the proceedings that it was, in fact, almost impossible for him to have done really well for the Defendant in such a complicated case. For all that Dr Kenealy was no match for the Crown's Counsel and the Claimant's case was very badly served by Dr Kenealy's outrageous conduct, even though it was motivated by a passionate belief in the Claimant and an equally passionate belief in the Court's prejudice against the Claimant. The extreme length of the case, too, could hardly have been conducive to a really competent trial. Judge Mellor, the senior judge at the trial, remarked sadly on the 69th day of the trial that "human life is not long enough to try these cases." And this was at a time when he had another 50 working days yet to come!

What was more, by the fortieth day of the trial the Claimant's money had all gone again. All the money he and his supporters had raised on their triumphant tour of England had been spent, and Holmes, the Claimant's first solicitor, had reappeared on the scene, now helping the prosecution!

To appreciate the extreme length of the trial it is only necessary to refer to the length of the speeches of the lawyers involved. Dr Kenealy spoke for a month in opening the Claimant's defence; his closing speech lasted from the beginning of December to the 14th January the following year. The prosecution's closing address lasted a fortnight and the Judge's summing-up a month!

Yet however long the Court and its officers had taken, at least the Jury came to its decision with despatch: they took only half an hour to find the Defendant guilty of both the perjuries which had been alleged against him. He was deliberately lying, they decided, when he said he was Roger Tichborne. They also decided he was lying deliberately when he said he had seduced Katherine, now the Lady Radcliffe. The Judge sentenced him to seven years' penal servitude on each count, a total of 14 years' imprisonment.

This was not the end of the bother by any means. Punch had earlier had a cartoon in its paper representing John Bull carrying the enormous bulk of the

Claimant on his back through a crowd of people carrying posters showing the serious concerns of the day, such as "Politics", "Education", "Army Reform", "The Irish Question", and John Bull is saying "I can't be expected to attend to any of you with this 'interesting topic' on my shoulders!"

Even the imprisonment of the Claimant did not stifle the continuing argument, and this despite Queen Victoria's obvious approval of the verdict, for she sent a telegram to Lady Radcliffe congratulating her on the vindication of her honour by the Court's decision. Disraeli, the Prime Minister, as his wife had taken such an avid interest throughout the Tichborne cases, rather more daringly presented her with a portrait of the Claimant as a memento of her consuming interest.

The cartoonists and pamphleteers of the day had lost their most popular subject. One last pamphlet, however, put the popular view in seven execrable verses when it was published at the conclusion of the trial and called "We'll not forget POOR ROGER now". Two of the verses were:

A deal of sympathy and humbug,
Was got up for Cousin Kate.
You may abuse the lower classes,
But mind you do not touch the great,
That they are angels dropped from heaven,
Divorce court trials will prove to you,
But then of course you must excuse them,
Because they've nothing else to do.

Then jolly good luck to brave Kenealy,
Their threats he did not care one jot,
Though he had five to one against him,
His voice was heard above the lot,
They may call the Claimant an imposter,
A lump of fat – the Counsel bawl,
But it is the universal feeling,
That he is the right man after all.

Within a month or two of the verdict Parliament passed the Tichborne Estates Act to allow the Trustees to pay the costs of the previous civil case out of the Tichborne Estate. It had cost them £92,000. For the prosecution of the Claimant it had cost the country £150,000.

The Tichborne Estates Act did not allow the immediate sale of Upton House and it was let until, finally, it passed from the Tichbornes to Mr W W Llewellin in 1901 when with some 930 acres of land, it was sold for £18,110.

By the time Upton House was sold by the Tichbornes the Claimant, convict No 10539, had left Portsea prison, his previous great bulk of 28 stones now reduced to 10 stones, but in much better general health. However, fourteen years later in

Queen Victoria sent a telegram to Lady Radcliffe congratulating her. Benjamin Disraeli,
the Prime Minister, presented his wife with a portrait of the Claimant.

1898 he died in penury in Marylebone where he had lived with his second wife. Then, despite the 20 years or so since his trial, over 5,000 people attended his funeral at Paddington Cemetery. His coffin, was inscribed "Sir Roger Charles Doughty Tichborne", and the local undertaker carried out the funeral arrangements free of cost.

The Claimant's death left many still wondering about various aspects of the case but with his old Counsel Kenealy dead there was only one who still campaigned vigorously in his cause and that was his daughter Teresa who had come with the Claimant as a baby from Australia. In 1912 she threatened to shoot Joseph Tichborne at his marriage and was imprisoned for it in Holloway. She was back in Holloway in 1924 for threatening to shoot Sir George Lewis. But mainly she sold flowers in Bond Street or outside Joseph Tichborne's flat, her name written in large letters on her basket. Later she used to go to Tichborne Park to get help from the family, and later still, it was thought, was supported by the Tichborne family through the Parish priest at Tunbridge Wells, where she lived until September 1939, and where at the age of 72, she died.

There have been many attempts to give a satisfactory answer to the many questions which arose from the Tichborne cases. Nearly everybody believed that there was much more to the case than was revealed. One of the more canvassed explanations appeared in the Cornhill Magazine in 1929. The author asserted that what had happened was that when George Orton of Wapping, the man whom the Claimant had tried to visit on his first days in England, was in financial difficulties his wife had taken a job as housekeeper at Upton House. While she was there the unhappily married James Tichborne had seduced her and the Claimant was the result of this liaison. Perhaps not surprisingly (the story went on) the child had never got on with George Orton and had therefore been only too happy to get away to sea but, before he had run away, he had been told of his Tichborne origins.

The author of this story professed that the first Mr W Llewellin had told him the story and that Mr Llewellin had previously heard it from the Tichborne lawyers. Moreover, it was said Mr Llewellin had found a letter at Upton House from George Orton to James Tichborne thanking him for a present which James Tichborne had sent him on the birth of the boy.

On being asked about this story when it appeared in the Cornhill, however, Lord Llewellin discounted it. He said that he had often discussed the Tichborne case with his father and, had his father had any knowledge of the things attributed to him in the article, Lord Llewellin was quite sure his father would have mentioned them to him - and his father had never referred to anything of this kind.

After Mr and Mrs W Llewellin came to live at Upton House it must have seemed that it was still not a lucky house for, a few years later, Mrs Llewellin was killed in a motor car accident near to the Willett Arms in the northern part of Poole. However, in 1908, Mr Llewellin married a second time to Mrs Ada Gaskell, a second cousin of his first wife who had herself lost her husband.

The families had known each other for a long time and the second Mrs Llewellin brought her own children to Upton House and they and the three Llewellin children were brought up happily together by her and Mr Llewellin.

Mr Llewellin's elder son, Mr W W Llewellin, entered the prison service and was the Governor of Borstal prisons including the first "open" Borstal, the "North Sea Camp", which he established at Freiston in Lincoln.

Mr J J Llewellin, the younger son, had a most distinguished public career. In the Great War of 1914-18 he served in the Dorset Royal Garrison Artillery in France and elsewhere. He became a barrister but his interest was in politics, and he entered the House of Commons as the Member for Uxbridge in 1929.

Eight years later he was appointed Civil Lord of the Admiralty and held this post until 1939. In 1940, when Lord Beaverbrook was made Minister of Aircraft Production by Winston Churchill, Mr Llewellin was appointed to serve with Lord Beaverbrook and to be responsible for the Ministry in the House of Commons and, when Lord Beaverbrook relinquished the post, Mr Llewellin took over all the responsibilities of the Ministry. Later, in 1942, Mr Llewellin served as President of the Board of Trade and, from 1943 to 1945 he was Minister of Food after Lord Woolton's period of office.

During this War period Mr Llewellin liked to return to Upton House whenever his duties permitted and many distinguished guests accompanied him or followed him down to Poole. Lord Frazer whose Home Fleet finally sunk the Scharnhorst, the German battle-cruiser, when escorting a vital convoy of supply ships going to Russia, and Harry Hopkins, Roosevelt's closet confidant and head of the Lend-Lease Administration, were only two of the very many distinguished guests and visitors to Upton House in those war days.

In 1945 Mr Llewellin was made Baron Llewellin of Upton and, in 1953, he was appointed Governor-General of the New Federation of Rhodesia and Nyasaland. Lord Llewellin had not married and his sister Miss Mary Llewellin accompanied him in this duty.

Lord Llewellin GBE PC MC TD was Governor-General of the Federation until his death in 1957.

Miss Mary Llewellin had herself a most distinguished career in local government. She served on the Poole Council from 1937 to 1954 as well as on the local bench of Magistrates. She was the first woman to be elected as Sheriff of Poole and, when in 1951 she was elected the 382nd Mayor of the Borough and County of the Town of Poole, she was the first lady Mayor the town had ever had.

In 1961 Mr W W Llewellin gave Upton House and the grounds immediately surrounding the house to the Poole Corporation. At that time the Corporation could see no immediate public use for the house and let it to His Royal Highness Carol of Hohenzollern, Prince of Roumania.

This lease, however, was not a successful solution of the problem of the future use of Upton House even for its new tenant and despite the fact that a son was born to the Prince and the Princess while they were living there. The Council, too, were criticised for not opening the property to the public but, for their part, they were concerned to find a beneficial use for the mansion if the grounds were opened to the public as well as the completion of major road works which would make the exit on to the main road safe for public use. However, before the road works were completed, the lease was formally surrendered by Prince Carol on the last day of 1969 and another unhappy chapter of Upton House's history had ended.

Since that time the property has been maintained as well as it could be while it was unoccupied, and with the main road works completed the grounds have recently been restored and remodelled to allow them to be opened to the public. Now, as many people stroll under the fine old trees of the park, perhaps they should listen carefully for the sounds of laughter and crying from the Mansion, for surely few houses have seen more gaiety or more tears.

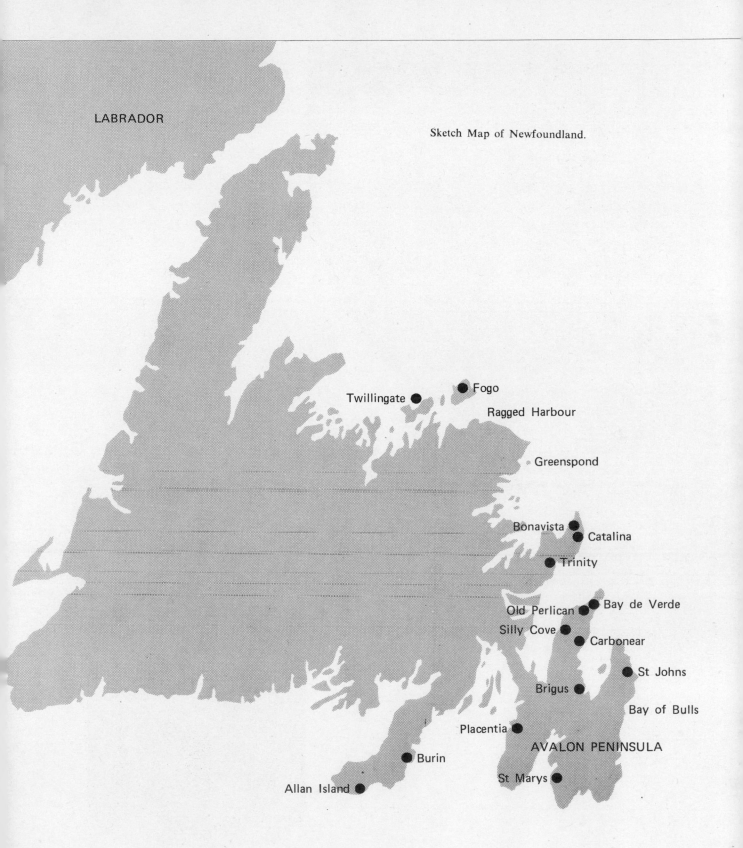

LABRADOR

Sketch Map of Newfoundland.

Fogo

Twillingate

Ragged Harbour

Greenspond

Bonavista

Catalina

Trinity

Bay de Verde

Old Perlican

Silly Cove

Carbonear

St Johns

Brigus

Bay of Bulls

Placentia

AVALON PENINSULA

Burin

St Marys

Allan Island

53

Thompson

NIL CONSCIRE SIBI

LUCEM SPERO

Kemp

The Poole Mansion

The few Poole merchants who left Poole to establish themselves as merchants in other ports seldom returned to Dorset. For all that, some of them remembered their early days in Poole with affection. One such merchant, one of the very earliest to leave Poole was Robert Rogers, whose family was otherwise firmly rooted in Bryanston and Poole, who set himself up as a merchant in London. There he became a most successful leather merchant, a member of the City of London Livery Company of Leather Sellers and made a fortune in the trade. When he died in 1601 he left the money for the Poole Corporation to erect almshouses in West Street which remained there for over 300 years. Even today he is still remembered by Rogers House, the offices recently built near the site of his old almshouses.

The only Poole merchant to return to live in Poole in Merchant Prince style was Peter Thompson. He returned to Poole to build and live in the Mansion house in Market Street which became known as the Poole Mansion.

Peter Thompson was the son of one of Poole's captains who had been mainly concerned in the trade with the American colonists in Carolina. For all that he had, like most Poole mariners, been also involved in the Newfoundland trade for, even when he was over 60 years old, his opinion was being canvassed in 1762 as to whether the French Army, then landed at the Bay of Bulls in Newfoundland, were likely to be able to drag their cannons overland to attack the British garrison at St John's. Peter Thompson knew the possible route well for he had himself walked over it in his youth and remembered vividly the "intolerably bad road, very hilly and many swampy, morass valleys". Peter Thompson's evidence, though still pertinent so far as the French cannon were concerned, was not then so relevant as to troop movements and needed supplementing by further and up-to-date evidence of another famous Poole mariner, Capt Taverner, who was able to say that as soon as the French landed at the Bay of Bulls they had set the Irish to cut down bushes and tree branches to make the road passable to their grenadiers. (In fact this is what the French did shortly afterwards, and took and sacked St John's despite the lack of cannon and despite the British garrison at St John's.)

Peter Thompson was not a burgess of Poole when he was young for, although he was of a family famous as ships' captains, he was a third son. Moreover, his elder brother James had already left Poole and set himself up as a merchant in London, and Peter left Poole in 1720 to join him in the merchanting business which he had established between London and Hamburg and, no doubt, Peter's previous experience in the Newfoundland trade on behalf of his uncle, another James Thompson, stood him in good stead.

In 1736 his brother James took Peter Thompson into partnership with him and it was about this time that Peter Thompson's fortunes rose dramatically for three years later his uncle James died in Poole leaving his Poole property to Peter Thompson and, a year later, his brother James died and, after his burial at St James church in Poole, Peter Thompson found himself the sole owner of the thriving Hamburg merchanting business in London as well as a property owner in Poole.

Peter Thompson was then rich and lived in Mill Street, Bermondsey, Surrey, and prospered both in his trade and in his social standing in Surrey. He was made a Justice of the Peace for Bermondsey and, a few years later, when Peter Thompson was 46 years old, it was in acknowledgement of his success elsewhere that the Poole Corporation at last elected him a free burgess of Poole. This was on 9th June, 1744, for Peter Thompson, like all good historians, kept the letter from the Town Clerk, Mr W Damen, telling him of his unanimous election as a burgess with others who had been proposed for burgesship at the meeting. The Town Clerk added that he wished one of them had been omitted, "but I make no Doubt, but we shall be able to keep some people a little to order and behaviour." The Town Clerk also wrote that the Mayor, John Lester, had been told that John Masters, the other new burgess who was to be kept "a little to order", intended to "Treat all his brethren as soon as he returned from London" and the Town Clerk thought that it might be a good idea for Mr Thompson, as a new burgess, to join with Mr Masters and make it a "hansom Treat". In fact Mr Damen, as any good Town Clerk would do, had already checked with the other new and opulent burgess and he was able to add that this proposal for a handsome repast "would be very agreeable to Mr Masters"!

The following year, in 1745, Peter Thompson was chosen as the High Sheriff of Surrey and, that same year, it fell to his lot to present the King with a Memorial from the inhabitants of Surrey applauding the King's action in suppressing the Jacobite revolt in Scotland. It was not unusual in those days for a monarch, pleased with the sentiments of such a Memorial, to honour the presenter of it, and Peter Thompson was dubbed Sir Peter Thompson.

This was not the end of Sir Peter's successes. A couple of years later he was elected as a Member of Parliament for St Albans but, although he remained in the House of Commons for seven years, he had been making his plans to retire from business and return to his native town of Poole even before he had become a Member of Parliament.

He bought some two acres of land straddling Pillory Street (later embodied in a lengthened Market Street) which previously had been known as Green Close, and engaged the famous Dorset builders, the Bastard Brothers of Blandford, to build him a mansion on the eastern portion of this land.

It was this new mansion which became known as "The Poole Mansion", and is possibly the best of the mansions built in the old town of Poole. Certainly, it was fortunate in its siting. Mansions in High Street, where many of them were built,

Sir Peter Thompson when living in Surrey.

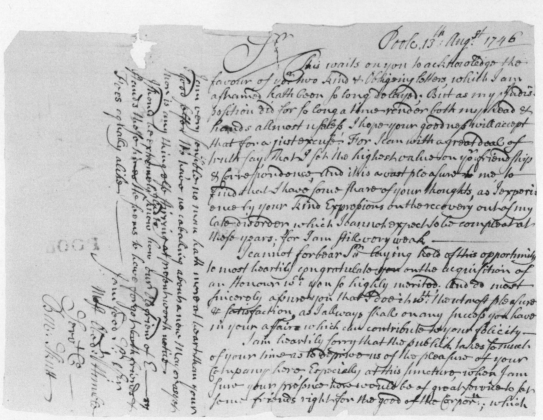

The original letter to Sir Peter Thompson from Benjamin Skutt some four years after he had last been Mayor of Poole.

57

were sometimes demolished for road widening, like the Spurriers' old property was in 1831 or, more often, they were ruined by having their lower floors gutted for conversion into shops when the centre of Poole's commerce moved from Market Street to High Street in the 19th century.

The photograph of John Bastard's letter to Sir Peter shows that even in those days there were the usual disputes and delays in the final settlement and payment for building work. It seems, too, that Sir Peter felt that John Bastard had put in his account so quickly because John Bastard, having heard that he was ill, feared he would die before he was paid. It also shows that John Bastard's literary abilities were no match for his expertise as a Master Builder. The letter read:

> To   Sr. Petter Thompson,
>   Member of Parliament
>   at his house in Southwark, London,
>
> Blandford ye 6th July 1752
>
> *Yours of ye 30th last past I receiv'd and have as you desier'd expain'd ye manner of mesuring naked flooring.*
>
> *As to ye strong fears I had during your late il'ness I know noathing of, nor did I know you was ill, till by your letter of ye 31st of December you told me so. Nor had I aney oather thought or meaning in Desiring ye account to be settled – but ye good old proverb, i.e. Short Reckonings make Long Friends.*
>
> *As to ye mesuering naked flooring is no more than supperfishial mesuer, the dimentions you have, or lengths and bredths. Ye way ye beams ar the dimentions, ar taken 12 inches into ye walls, and ye Joyst lye, is 6 in. into ye walls, this multeyplied one by ye other gives ye sqaurs.*
>
> *As to cuing ye timber you know very well I told you that I never had dun aney in that manner, nor is there any shuch method usd; or heard of here – the prise pr square in adapted to ye goodness of ye work, and ye materials usd in it. And your carpenter when we was together at your house, agreed that if naked flooring was dun well it was worth 40s pr sqr in London, and I'm shure its worth, and costs a great deal more here, than thear. We have no choice of timber, and mostly small and badly squard, nails we have from London, and hindorans by masens etc.*
>
> *You nor nobodey Else can say but yours is dun strong and well, and have had time to prove it – the house stands bleak, and much exposd. And I think there never was a house beter defended against storms nor more care taken in Rooffing, and lead work. I never saw nor hard of a drop that came in aney whar.*
>
> *I shall be very willing to have ye account setteld but as to ye paying ye ballance I'm very Indiferent, that may be as you pleas. I have as you directed sent ye bills of whar's dun sins ye last account was deliverd you, and have sent you ye dimentions, and measuers of all ye painting thats now dun.*

Blandford ye 6th July 1752

Yours of ye 30th Last past I recevd, and have as
you desird explaind ye maner of mesuring naked
flooring —
as to ye strong fears I had durek your Late Illness
I know noathing of nar did I know you was Ill, till
by your Leter of ye 31th of December you told me so —
Nor had I eney other though or meaning in Desireing
ye acount to be setteld — but ye good old proverb is —
{ short Reckonings, make Long friends }

As to ye mesuring naked flooring is no more than super-
-ficshial mesner, the dimentions you have, or Lengths
and bredths, ye way ye beams or ye dimentions, ar takon
12 inches into ye walls, and ye way ye Joyst Lye, is 6
into ye walls, thes multey p Cled one by ye other gives ye
squars —

As to Cubing ye timber you know very well I told you that
I neber hed dun eney in that maner, nor is there my
Shred methoad ussd or Heard of here — the priz
ye squar — is adapted to ye goodness of ye work, &
ye materials usd in it — and your Carpenter when
we was together at your house, agreed that ye
naked flooring was dun well it was worth 40s
ye squar in London, and Im shure its worth, and Costs
a great deal more here, than thear. We have no Choise
of timber, and mostly smale & badly squard, nall we
have from London, and hinderans of masens, &c —

you nor nobodey else Can say but yours is dun strong
and well, and have had time to prove it — the hous
stands bleak, and much exposd and I think ther
never was a house beter defended against storms
nor more Care takon in Roofing and Lead work —
I never saw nor hard of a drop that Came in eney
whare —

I shall be very willing to have ye acount setteld, but
as to ye paying ye ballance Im very Indiferent that
may be as you pleas. I have as you directed sent
you ye bills of whats dun sins ye Last acount was
deliverd you & have sent you ye dimentions, and
mesures of ye painting thats now dun

I hant yet had time to Inrich ye Cornishes of ye Rooms
now painted, in ye maner they was dun before. So hant Charg
that artical, that may be Chargd when dun —

as to this methoad I now use, and is usd by Every bodey in this
Cuntrey was Shewn me—first by Mr John Jeames of Greenwick &
he was allowd to be as good a Carpenter as eney in his time, & he
was Often at ower hoase, and this is ye methoad, Mr Hassroney have
Latly Published in his book, of firme himself
your humble servt John Bastar

The original envelope and letter of 8 July 1752 from John Bastard to Sir Peter Thompson.

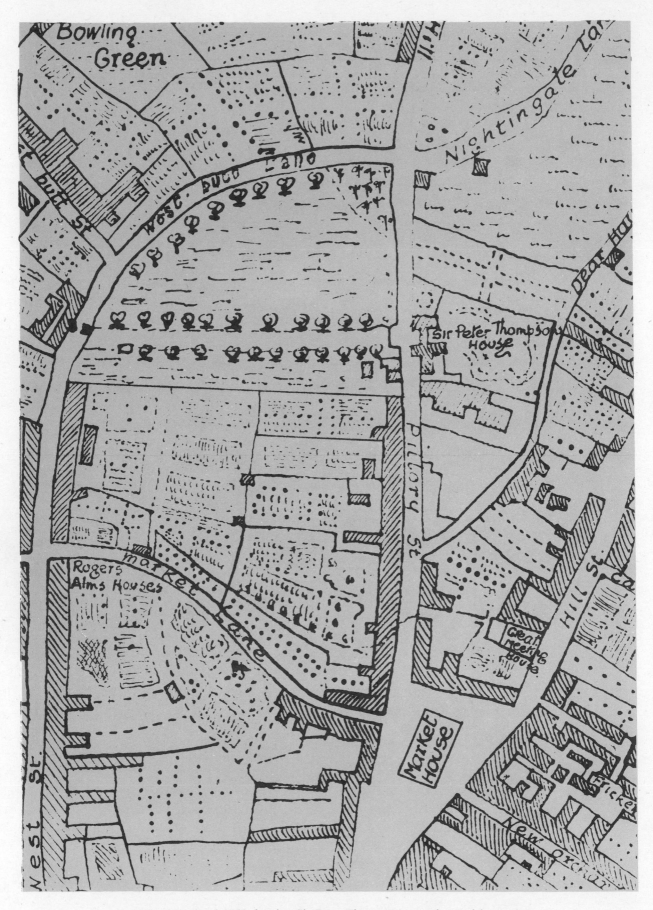

Map of Poole of 1756 showing Sir Peter Thompson's mansion and its gardens.

Sir Peter Thompson at Poole

One of the Rev Hutchins's letters to Sir Peter
while he was helping with the 'History of Dorset'.
The 'Coker' referred to in the letter was
a manuscript about Dorset, written in 1732
by Thomas Coker, Surveyor of Dorset, which
Sir Peter owned and had lent to the Rev Hutchins.

61

I han't yet had time to Inrish ye cornishes of ye 3 Rooms now painted, in ye manner they was dun before. So han't charg'd that artical, that may be char'd when dun.

As to this method I now use, and is us'd be every bodey in this cuntry was shown me ferst by Mr John James of Greenwich, and he was alow's to be as good a carpenter az aney in his time, and he was Oaften at ower house. And this is the method Mr Halfpeney have latly published in his book of farme houses.

Yours humble servt
(sgd) John Bastard

On the completion of his mansion, Sir Peter had the usual wall erected round the immediate garden of the house, and had the garden set out with paths and lawns. But it was the land on the western side of Pillory Street which allowed him scope to set off the mansion to its best effect. He had this large area of land enclosed by fine, ornamental wrought-iron railings. Then he had a carriageway laid with an avenue of trees beside it leading to the house from West Butt Lane. He had that garden landscaped, the central feature being a small ornamental lake whose water was fed by a series of pipes from the sea in Holes Bay.

Sir Peter Thompson retired to live permanently in his new mansion in 1763. His widowed sister came to live with him to act as his housekeeper, and he spent his retirement taking a great interest in local affairs and in Poole's elections (for, of course, he had had considerable personal experience of these) and in collecting books, manuscripts and ancient records of Poole and its history. On his death Sir Peter left this invaluable collection of Poole records to his nephew, Captain Peter Thompson, an officer in the grenadiers of the Surrey militia, who sold some of the books to Ralph Willett of Merley, but the greater part of the collection was not disposed of until 1825 when it was sold by auction in London. Unfortunately now the only trace of this unique accumulation is in the pages of Hutchins's "History of Dorset", for Sir Peter gave a great deal of help to Rev Hutchins in the preparation of his famous book.

Sir Peter and his sister, Mrs Haselden, died within four days of each other in October 1770 and were buried together in St James's Churchyard near to the spot where Sir Peter's elder brother and Mrs Haselden's husband had been buried a few years earlier.

For a time the house remained unoccupied and its contents undisturbed and, although the house had eventually been let for a few years, it was not until 1788 that it was at last sold – and then to another of Poole's merchants, George Kemp, who bought it for £6,000.

The Kemps in a number of ways were very different from the usual Newfound-land merchant operating out of the port of Poole. For one thing, they took no part in the administration of the town's affairs. In the early days this was because, although they must have been burgesses of the town, they lived at Beaulieu and Christchurch. Therefore, they were 'outburgesses' whose only privilege apart from being able to trade from the port, was that they were able to vote in the election of Poole's two Members of Parliament.

The family, although owning land in the Isle of Wight and in the western half of Hampshire, originated in Kent where its members had had most distinguished careers in the Church. One, John Kemp, had been Archbishop of Canterbury. His canopied tomb is still to be seen in Canterbury Cathedral. But this was all before the 16th century. Edward Kemp moved his family into west Hampshire late in that century and lived there long enough to have made a great impression on the local people for, on his death in 1605, a brass was placed in Beaulieu Church to commemorate him. His son Thomas must later have moved further west in the county, because he obtained considerable distinction in Christchurch. He was Mayor there three times between 1625 and 1640, as well as sitting in the House of Commons as Member of Parliament representing Christchurch and Lymington.

With such a background it therefore seems strange that later members of the Kemp family should take to the arduous trade of mariners, skippers and finally merchants in the Poole-Newfoundland trade, but that is what they did.

They must, too, have entered the trade before the end of the 17th century, for by 1725 they were already merchants of sufficient standing to be listed with the five famous firms of Fryer, Gosse & Pack, Pike, Green and Slade as the merchants trading from Carbonear in Newfoundland.

For all that, James Kemp was still a working ship's captain in 1739 when his ship the *Neptune* of 151 tons, the largest of some twenty ships then in the port, was caught by a Government "Embargo Warrant". This was a device by which the Government kept ships in port usually, as in this case, to give its Press Gangs time forcibly to enlist trained mariners into the Royal Navy before the fishing ships had sailed. On this occasion, for instance James Kemp not only lost precious fishing time as he was caught in port by the Embargo, but lost two of his experienced sailors to the Navy before he was eventually allowed to sail out of Poole.

Despite the fact that the bulk of the sailors of the Royal Navy were trained in the service of the merchants of Poole and Dartmouth, the Navy gave little or no priority in time of war to the protection of the fleet of ships and the mariners involved in the trade. In 1761, for instance, the Navy told the merchants it could give their fishing fleet no protection from the marauding French Navy and privateers on their return from Newfoundland in the autumn of that year. The merchants were given permission however, to arm one of their own ships at their own expense to escort their fleet of ships back to Europe. The ship which the merchants chose for the conversion had to be fast and manoeuvrable, and it was therefore a compliment to the Kemp's ship-building yards which, with the Spurriers provided many of the Poole ships and fishing boats from the yards they had established in Newfoundland, that it was the Kemp's *Neptune* which was chosen for the purpose. The *Neptune* had 20 guns installed in her and a complement of 125 men and the Navy seconded one of its Lieutenants to take charge of her.

Tomb of John Kemp in Canterbury Cathedral.

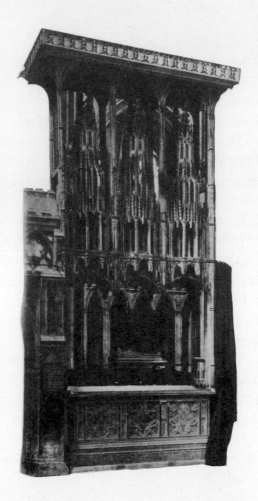

Arms of the Kemp family, surmounted by the Kemp Crest, on a wreath.

THE KEMP FAMILY OF OLLANTIGH

"Lo! all our Pomp of yesterday, is one with Nineveh and Tyre" ✸ ✸
IF—you can walk with kings, nor lose the common touch, you'll be a man."
(Kipling.)

Chapter I

THE first Kemp, known as owner of the Manor of Ollan tigh, in the Parish or Town of Wye, Kent, was Ralph Kemp, then called Radalphus De Campis, during the reign of Edward I, in 1283. He died in 1313 and left a son John.

Sir John Kemp, son of Ralph, inherited Ollantigh and married Agnes, daughter of Sir Thomas Alden; they left a son Peter.

Sir Peter Kemp, son of Sir John, is described as living at Wye in 1352. He left a son Thomas.

The first page of 'The Kemps of Ollantigh and Kemps of Poole" by Dr George Kemp IV, Seattle, USA 1939.

On James Kemp's death his firm was taken over by Martin Kemp who moved from Christchurch to live in Poole, and it was there that in 1755 he married Mary Welch of Lymington.

The family had by this time left the Anglican Church in which their ancestors had had such distinguished roles. Martin Kemp had joined the Congregational Church in Poole which had a chapel in Hill Street just above the site where the new Guildhall was to be built a few years later. It was probably through Martin Kemp leaving the Anglican Church that the Kemps now living in Poole still took no part in the affairs of the Poole Corporation for, until 1828 when Parliament repealed the Corporation Act of 1661, to be eligible to become Mayor, Sheriff or take any other office in the Corporation's service, the burgess had to have taken the sacrament in the Church of England within a year of his taking office.

It was, in fact, this very point which first started the quarrels arising within the Congregational Church in Poole at this time. Many of those converted to the Congregational Church at that time were members of the Poole Corporation and they wished to take Communion in St James Church from time to time so that they could comply with the provisions of the Act and achieve or retain the offices in the Corporation's service. The other Congregationalists, however, not illogically, considered that men thus wanting a foot in each camp could hardly be admitted to full membership of the Congregational Church.

Such disputes were very small beer compared with the passion of the later quarrels which developed in the Congregational Church just after Martin Kemp had joined it. These quarrels centred round the theological argument as to the relationship between God, Jesus Christ and the Holy Ghost. A number of the "proprietors" of the Church in whom its management was vested had, one can only assume, been persuaded by a previous pastor that the Trinity were not quite of "one substance"; that, although Jesus Christ was begotten before time and was co-eternal, God alone was completely supreme. In fact, these Poole Congregationalists with others in the country had in the middle of the 17th century, revived the very first heresy of the Catholic Church, propounded by Arius, a Libyan, who died in AD 336, and whose heresy was generally believed to have been extinct and forgotten by the end of the fourth century!

In 1759, on the death of a number of the other "proprietors" of the Church, the "Arians" among the Congregation suddenly found they had a majority in the Church. They decided to act quickly while they were technically in this strong position. They locked the pastor out of his own Church and took possession of it against all the conventional Congregationalists and the pastor.

The surprising thing was that, though many of the leading Poole families were thus unceremoniously hustled out of what they had thought was their Church, and though they seemed to have an extremely good case at law to recover it, they decided not to take their quarrels to the Courts. Under the lead of Martin Kemp, now made Deacon, the Linthornes, the Durells, the Ledgards, the Gillinghams, the Millers and other leading Poole families decided to leave the old chapel to the "Arians" and build themselves a new chapel in Leg Lane (Lagland Street). The dispossessed Congregationalists successfully accomplished this, leaving the "Arians" to their seized chapel which they promptly renamed "The Unitarian Chapel", in accordance with their adopted doctrine, and as such it remained. It was sited to the north of the Guildhall behind the old Police Station and the Green Market of the Corporation in Hill Street. Although the rebuilt building was damaged by the bomb which demolished the old Police Station (which had been used for "slipper baths" since 1907) it remained there until about seven years ago when it was demolished by the Corporation so that its site could form part of the Salvation Army's new headquarters in Poole.

Happily for the new Independent Church, Martin Kemp was able to continue as Deacon for the next twelve years until the Church had become established and a new, lively and popular pastor, the Rev Edward Ashburner, had been appointed. When Martin Kemp died suddenly in 1772, therefore, the Church was firmly established and well able to survive without him.

However, this was far from the position with his own business. His death at the age of 48 made it very questionable whether his firm could survive. His eldest son, George, was then barely 16 years old and had not started his training for the trade, let alone being able to take over the management of such a complicated business.

This problem often occurred in those early days before the invention of the "Company" which, having a corporate identity of its own, could survive the merchant's death. In those days the nearest the merchants could come to making a company of their business was to go into partnership with other merchants, but such an arrangement often raised more problems than it cured. In the early days, therefore, the survival of a merchanting business depended very greatly on the orderly succession of sons who were able and willing to take on the business.

In the absence of such a son, the only way for the business to continue on the death of a merchant was for the executors to take it on, but this was only possible when the executors had both the ability and time to do so and, normally, only then if they could forsee a permanent solution in the reasonable future. Usually, therefore, in the absence of an heir being immediately available, it was just a matter of the executors dividing up the business between the beneficiaries or selling the business quickly while there was still something to sell.

On Martin Kemp's death, therefore, it must have been a very worrying time for his wife, Mary Kemp for, apart from her concern as to her husband's business and her future income, she was left with four children, George, John, Mary and James to bring up, and was also five months pregnant of a further child. On the other hand she was lucky in that her own family of the Welch's were well able to give her support. Her father and brother, who were Martin Kemp's executors, were bankers in the City of London. Her brother, George Welch, was unmarried and therefore free from any concerns of his own family and, with his father, agreed to continue Martin Kemp's business as executors until his nephews could grow up and be trained to take it over themselves.

George Welch, in taking on the general management of the Kemp business, appointed the very experienced Newfoundland trader, John Green of Poole, as manager of the business jointly with a banker, John Holden of London, presumably a member of the Welch banking firm.

On Martin Kemp's death in 1772 the Kemp business was not one of the larger businesses in Newfoundland and, although by general consent the temporary managers of the Kemp business had done very well for the Kemp children in keeping the business in being and successful, it was still only moderate in size when George and his brother James took it back from the Executors. In 1785, for instance, when the Board of Trade had a report of the more important merchants in Newfoundland, although nineteen of the Poole merchants were listed in this report, the Kemp business did not rate a mention among the forty-five "strongest merchants" then operating in Newfoundland.

It was, though, in this period when the firm was being carried on by the Executors and the two boys, George and James, were growing up and being trained in the trade, that prudent management laid the foundations of the firm's later growth. George and James both served their apprenticeship in the trade and George, if not James also, had for a period supervised the Newfoundland end of the business.

Once back in Poole, George, the eldest son, quickly concerned himself in his family's interest in the Church. He had always shared his family's deep religious belief, and he took a very active part in the affairs of the Independent Church in Lagland Street which his father had been instrumental in founding. In 1781, George, like his father before him, was made Deacon of the Church.

George and his brother James also took a very active part in the politics of Poole. Curiously, James was an ardent Tory and George was a staunch Whig. In fact later on George was made the leader of the Poole Whigs, a position he retained until 1835. The effect of the differing political opinions of the two brothers and business partners was that they regularly and methodically voted in the Poole elections, one vote for each of the Parties, and thereby usually managed to cancel each other's votes!

G & J Kemp, as the firm was now called, was far from the Merchant Prince class when they took back the business from their father's Executors. However, George Kemp had bought "The Poole Mansion" in 1788, on his marriage to Sarah Gosse, the daughter of one of the firm's suppliers, a cloth manufacturer of Ringwood and, shortly afterwards, he and his wife went to live there. Their marriage brought together two families which were both deeply concerned in the Newfoundland trade for Sarah Gosse's uncle, John Gosse, was the agent for G & J Kemp in Newfoundland; another uncle, Henry Gosse, worked for Benjamin Lester, the eminent Poole merchant, and Sarah's brother, Thomas, was the father of Philip Henry Gosse who, after being educated at Blandford Grammar School, worked first for George

Garland in Poole and afterwards for the Slades in Newfoundland before he became famous as a zoological writer.

By the 1790's it seemed that the Kemp brothers were then all but established in their businesses. George and James in their father's merchanting business in Newfoundland; John in one of Poole's ancillary trades, that of mercer, with premises in High Street and Martin, born four months after his father's death, brought up by George Welch as his own son, in training for George Welch's profession of banking.

In fact a few years later this youngest son, Martin Kemp, shortly after his 21st birthday, agreed with his uncle, who was unmarried and had no heir of his own, to add his uncle's surname to his own, and arrangements were made for him to join the thriving banking firm of George Welch Ledgard of Poole and Ringwood then owned and run by George Welch Ledgard, whose own mother had probably been related to the Welch's of Christchurch.

Martin Kemp's change of name was, of course, properly authenticated. George Welch paid £500 for the Royal Licence for this to take place, and it was announced in the *London Gazette* on 16 May 1795. The official announcement read:

"The King has been pleased to grant unto Martin Kemp of Tower Hill, London, son of Martin Kemp of Poole, Dorset, his Royal Licence that he and his issue may take the surname of Welch in addition to that of Kemp in compliance with the wish of his maternal uncle, George Welch, Esquire, of the City of London, Banker".

It is unlikely that there had been any doubts in the minds of the Kemp brothers that they were the natural heirs to their unmarried uncle's estate, for he had so long acted as their guardian. Had they previously entertained any doubts on this score they would probably have been set at rest by their uncle's concern that their younger brother Martin should take his name of Welch.

It therefore came as a great shock to the Kemp brothers only a few months afterwards to be told that their uncle intended to marry Margaret Evans, a woman younger than himself for, not only did this mean that George Welch would be called upon to make a marriage settlement in her favour, but there was now the possibility of George Welch having children of his own who would naturally become his heirs in lieu of themselves.

George Welch was however, clearly conscious of the effect his intended marriage would have on his nephews and he took what he thought to be reasonable steps to tell them of his intention and to appease their expectations. In December 1795 he entered into a formal Deed of Gift with the four Kemp brothers, giving each of them his Bond to pay them £5,000 as well as giving to them various properties in Poole and London. To George Kemp, he specifically gave "the Deeds relating to the premises at Poole purchased by Geo: Kemp with the money of Geo: Welch".

However, it is clear that Margaret Evans, George Welch's bride and her family, on hearing of the dispositions which her new husband had made to his nephews just prior to their marriage early in 1796, considered his gifts to be much too generous to the Kemp brothers and unfair to her. One cannot help feeling sympathy for George Welch thus caught, in the first few days of his marriage, between the claims on his fortune from his new wife and her family on the one hand and from his nephews on the other.

What made it worse for George Welch was that neither side with a claim on his fortune was willing to help him gracefully out of his predicament. He wrote to George Kemp, the eldest Kemp brother, early in 1796, asking the brothers to agree to cancel the Deed of Gift made only a few weeks previously so that another Deed could be drawn up. George Kemp, the Deacon of the Independent Church of Poole for fifteen years, found his anger and frustration at this turn of events too strong for his charity. On 1 March 1796, he wrote the following letter to his uncle.

Hon^d Sir

I have just received yours of yesterday. You will very readily excuse me when I say the contents are not very agreeable. But we live in a world of change and I wish for Grace to say that the will of God be done.

It hurts me very much to perceive anything like a wish to have anything altered, and I trust that you will not desire it. Rather let me desire you to consider that if, after having again and again been taught to look upon all your Fortune as our own, if we loose half of it, it is enough.

I am so much hurt for the present I know not how to write; nor to attend upon my business. Surely, ever since I have had years of discretion, I have been a Slave, and now I am called to witness a new scene of trouble.

You will find by the memorandum paper which I left with you, that if you have one child there is to be five thousand pounds for it, which was your own proposal; if two or three children £9,000; If four £10,000; All this is separate and distinct from the £10,000 for Mrs Welch, and all of us are bound to see these things carried into effect.

You will see the propriety of getting the money together for those purposes in due time. But first of all you will pay off the Notes which constitute the first Gifts to your Nephews and my poor Sister.

You know that the Deed of Gift is secured by your bond, and Mr Smith was a witness to the same, and if anything is done to disturb the security it will make Void the contract in the marriage settlement. The Will is nothing more than a confirmation of the Deeds of Settlement.

I hope you will come down soon and put everything in a proper way to answer all the agreements made. I want nothing but what you may have thought right, and surely no part of Mrs Welch's family will attempt any thing to endanger her Settlement.

With grief,

I subscribe myself

(sgd) G Kemp.

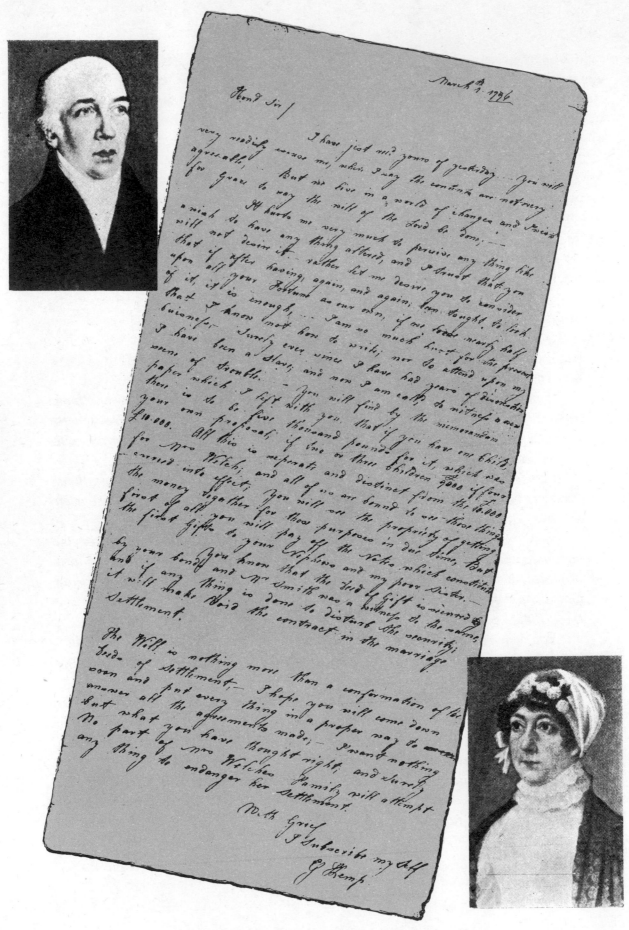

George Kemp, his letter of March 1796 and Sarah Gosse Kemp.

It took until 21 May that year to agree to new "Articles of Agreement" to settle the dispute. As the Deed embodying the agreement blandly stated "some Misunderstanding having taken Place with Respect to the Intention of the said Geo: Welch at the time of executing the Indenture of the 10 December 1795", it needed a further Deed of Gift to rectify the position.

By this Agreement the Kemp brothers agreed to return to George Welch all the "Bonds and Covenants and Notes and other Securities, Deeds, Papers and other Instruments" which George Welch had given them, excepting the Deeds of the Poole premises bought by George Kemp with George Welch's money, but it was stipulated that George Kemp would allow Rev E Ashburner and his wife to live in the house free of rent for the rest of their lives. The Articles also provided for each of the four brothers to receive £5,000, but this was subject to them paying to George Welch 3% interest on these amounts up to the date of his death. They were then to share a further £10,000 3% Annuities from the estate of the survivor of George Welch and his wife Margaret.

By this time George Kemp and his wife had had four children themselves, first two daughters, Sarah and Mary and then two boys, George and Henry. The two boys were sent away to boarding school at Weymouth in 1796 even though George was only 12 and Henry 7 years old. Henry seems not to have minded the separation as much as George who clearly from the letters he wrote home was none too happy with his enforced stay in Weymouth. On 16th August 1796, for instance, after he and Henry had been returned to Weymouth, George wrote the following letter to his parents:

> *Dear and Hon^d Parents*
>
> *An unexpected opportunity by Mr Wm Brown I was not willing to let slip especially how anxious you would be concerning us. Both Harry and myself are in good health and tolerable spirits and pretty well reconciled to our continuance at Weymouth.*
>
> *The Troops were review^d this morning by the King who set off this day early for that purpose.*
>
> *Weymouth is extremely lively:- the Streets exceedingly dusty and everybody remarkably busy – in doing what? Why truly nothing!*
>
> *With my Brother's and my own united duty.*
>
> > *Hon^d and Dear Parents*
> > *I remain, Very affectionately*
> > *Your dutiful Son*
> > *(sgd) G Kemp.*

It was, too, during these years that the business of G & J Kemp started its meteoric rise. The firm of their tutor and late Manager had on his death hit the same trouble as their own father's business had done. There were, however, in John

Green's case no executors able and willing to take over the business, nor were there in his case any heirs, then growing up, who would later be able to take it over. It had, therefore, logically been bought by William Pike, the other large Poole merchant in Conception Bay in Newfoundland. These two businesses had both separately been classified in 1785 as two of the "strongest merchants in Newfoundland". The new firm of Pike & Green was therefore very large, and it was this combined firm of two of the largest and longest established Poole firms in Newfoundland that were taken over by G & J Kemp just before the turn of the century. At one stroke, G & J Kemp had become one of the largest merchanting houses in Newfoundland.

G & J Kemp had by this successful business coup attained for their firm the business premises, the trade and the ships of William Pike and John and Young Green at Poole and at Carbonear in Conception Bay. If any of the Poole merchants were ever entitled to the title of "the millionaire firm of Poole" which was applied to various of the Poole firms from time to time it seemed in the early 1800's that it was the firm of G & J Kemp. They not only had achieved a large business in the supply to their own merchanting houses in Newfoundland which had a very large trade in fish but, at Burin, they built many ocean-going ships as well as many of the fishing boats for the "Planters", as the independent fishermen were called. In addition the firm supplied many goods to the independent traders of St John's.

Probably the most renowned of Kemps' ships was the *General Wolfe* whose skipper was Captain Tulloch. Early in the Napoleonic wars the *General Wolfe* was captured with its cargo of fish and seal oil in the Atlantic by a French privateer. Captain Tulloch and most of his crew were transferred to the French frigate as prisoners. Only the mate of the *General Wolfe* with one of its mariners and a young Newfoundland trainee were left aboard the *General Wolfe* to help sail the Poole vessel to France under the charge of a French officer and the prize crew of ten men who had been put aboard the *General Wolfe* by the captain of the French frigate.

It apparently did not occur to the French officer or his prize crew that their duty of sailing the *General Wolfe* back to Brest was anything but a routine job. At the main meal times nine of the prize crew messed together in the forward cabin leaving one of their number on deck at the wheel. At the same time the officer ate his meal alone in the captain's cabin midships, waited on by the boy trainee. The English mate and seaman were left on deck to carry out the orders of the French seaman at the wheel of the *General Wolfe*.

The mate of the Poole ship had noticed that the French officer always threw off his pistol belt as he sat down at the captain's table to eat his meals. It occurred to him, therefore, that he had a chance to recapture the ship if he could get the officer's pistols and somehow manage to keep the French prize crew below deck. He therefore secretly bored holes with a gimlet in the side of the fore and aft companionways so that when the covers of the companionways were pulled down nails could be slipped through the gimlet holes to fasten them down. Then, one day, when the boy had just given the French officer his meal, the mate gave a signal at which the boy seized the officer's belt with its two pistols and threw it up on to the deck where the mate was waiting. At the same time the seaman pushed the nails which the mate had provided him with through the holes made by the mate, and thus secured the scuttles.

The plot nearly failed as the French officer realised what was happening and running to the companionway, was able to clutch hold of the boy's feet as he dashed up towards the safety of the deck. Happily, the boy had got high enough for the mate on the deck to seize the boy's arms and, after a hectic tug-of-war between the French captain below hanging on grimly to the boy's boots and the Poole mate heaving the boy upward towards the deck the contest was eventually won by the mate as the boy's feet were dragged free of his boots by main force.

The mate, the seaman and the boy then alone on the deck and with eleven of their captors imprisoned below, sailed the *General Wolfe* with its cargo back into Poole where the grateful insurers of the vessel and its cargo presented the mate with the then very princely sum of 500 guineas, the seaman 100 and the young Newfoundland boy from Carbonear with 40 guineas.

The *General Wolfe* in fact must have originally been taken by surprise by the French for it was "an exceptionally smart vessel" able, shortly afterwards, in the second American War of Independence, when the American privateers were generally so successful against English shipping, to outsail an American privateer and escape with the provisions which it had bought in Quebec and were desperately needed in Carbonear.

Despite the frequent successes of the French and American privateers, the few years up to the battle of Waterloo in 1815 and for a short period thereafter were probably the most prosperous period of Newfoundland's history, for the Napoleonic Wars had closed the Scandinavian and Dutch fisheries. The Kemp firm shared fully in this prosperity. In addition to their successful general trade, the two Kemp brothers made a fortune in one single journey by two of their ships.

During the Peninsular War in 1810 when the Royal Navy was blockading the Spanish ports as part of the Government's strategy against Napoleon's efforts to keep his brother Joseph as King of Spain, Marshal Suchet, Napoleon's General, had overrun Southern Spain. The Royal Navy was stationed all along the Spanish coast to ensure that no supplies were landed which could fall into the hands of the French Army. The blockade was successful in that it effectively deprived Spain of its usual supplies of food, shortages of which were, of course, greatly accentuated by the demands of the invading armies and the lack of men even to produce the normal supplies of the Spanish countryside itself. Moreover the blockade effectively stopped the export of Spain's produce and, even their own reduced produce, especially wine, accumulated in the Spanish ports.

Thus, when two of the Kemps' ships evaded the blockade of the Royal Navy and made port there they were not only able to sell their cargo of cod at exorbitant prices but were able to buy the best wine extremely cheap. The two ships then successfully evaded the blockade again to come back to England. The Kemp brothers sent the vessels off to London where one of them went post haste to prepare to sell off their precious wine in small lots at the very highest of the prices then ruling, for the blockade had starved London of its usual supplies of wine.

However, at the end of the war with France, competition in the fisheries developed again as other nations resumed their fisheries. Scandinavian fishermen were particularly successful in the extension of the cod-fishing round the Lofoden Islands. Concessions were made to the French negotiators of the Peace at the end of the war, and the French Government encouraged their own fishermen by giving them bounties on the fish which they caught. To make matters even worse for the Poole merchants, the Spaniards put high duties on the cod imported into Spain. The result was that the Newfoundland fishery and merchants suffered a period of great depression. This meant that the immigrants living in Newfoundland could not all be supported by the reduced level of the trade, and it was thought that the Government would have to shift at least 10,000 of them away from the island. Bulley & Job, merchants in the Newfoundland trade from Teignmouth, in 1817, wrote to the Government in despair: "we shall take early measures such as prudence may dictate to retreat from the trade before we have lost all our property" unless the Government gave them immediate help.

At this time Edward Kemp, the eldest son of James Kemp, was the agent of G & J Kemp in Brigus. He wrote home in February 1817, to say his supplies were almost exhausted. Food, he reported, was already rationed, and there was barely enough to keep their crews alive until May. He feared that there would be a riot at the first sight of a provision ship sailing into the port.

Only a short time after writing this letter Edward Kemp was drowned, caught with his Poole crew (G Best, John Barnes, C Vayard, John Whitty and Dr Christed) in one of Newfoundland's treacherous squalls as they were crossing in an open boat from Brigus to the firm's other station at Carbonear.

This calamity was probably the final straw in making up the mind of George and James Kemp to draw out of the Newfoundland trade. Everything seemed now to be conspiring against them. George Kemp's wife, Sarah, had died in 1813 and, two years later, the 58 year old widower married again, to a 31 year old widow, Elizabeth Knight (née Pearce) who herself had already had children of her own.

This marriage upset George's four children. It affected his eldest son, George Junr, just as much as, 20 years earlier, his uncle's marriage to Margaret Evans had disconcerted his father. By that time George Junr had married the daughter of the local doctor, Richard Miller and, for a time, he lived in St James Rectory which was then awaiting a new Rector, and later in a house in High Street. He had worked in his father's 'counting house' in Poole but was soon to abandon thoughts of continuing in the trade. He was not well, and probably not thought strong enough for that rough training. A little later he left Poole to take up dairy farming at West Holme near Wareham. George Senior then had trouble with his daughter Mary who wished to marry a Poole apothecary whom her father considered totally unworthy of her, and he refused to agree to the marriage. After that it seems that life with the two families living together in the Poole Mansion became impossible. George Kemp decided that the only way in which his two families could live in peace was separately. He built Creekmoor House for Mary Kemp and her two unmarried sisters to move into, and he and his second wife and their children remained at the Poole Mansion.

Then suddenly, in 1824, the great firm of G & J Kemp was no more. The partners sold out to another large Newfoundland firm of Poole, the then combined firm of Fryer, Gosse & Pack. George was then 68 years old, James only a few years younger, and after Edward's death, none of their family were able or willing to consider taking on the business.

George Kemp Junr, who had returned to Poole from West Holme the year before, decided in 1828, to get out of England altogether. He himself was then 44 years old. There seemed no prospects in Poole for him. He could expect little more from his father, his second wife then being pregnant with her seventh child by George Kemp, so George Kemp Junr eventually turned down an offer of an important post in Tasmania and took his family to brave a six weeks journey through a stormy Atlantic to begin a new life. The following January he became an American citizen and, through him and the Poole doctor's daughter who was his wife, started a new and vigorous line of American Kemps from his new town of Augusta, Michigan, where they lived till their deaths in 1863.

Meanwhile in Poole the fortune of the senior partner in the great "millionaire" firm of G & J Kemp had apparently evaporated. Some of it no doubt had gone to set up George Kemp's large family. A considerable amount was lost in the catastrophic fall in the value of property in Poole and by houses being left vacant, caused by the decline in the Newfoundland trade, for it was said at one time that George Kemp owned nearly half of Poole. There was, too, of course, the decline in the Newfoundland trade itself which the Kemps' business must have felt even prior to 1824 when it was sold. Whatever the causes, George Kemp's fortune, estimated at not less than £250,000 a few years earlier, had been most seriously reduced by the 1830's.

For all that George Kemp was still the leader of the Poole Whigs, still the leader of the Nonconformists in Poole, and still one of the most respected men in the town. On more solemn occasions in the town he was known as the "aristocratic deacon", but on more mundane occasions the people of Poole referred to him as "Georgey" for, to the "modern" eyes of the early nineteenth century, his dress was most eccentric, being in the style more appropriate to that of his grandfather. According to Densham and Ogle's "Congregational Churches of Dorset" he wore "a black coat and small clothes, silk stockings, silver buckles shoes or hessian boots, and his silver locks, which were covered by a shovel hat, were tied pig-tail fashion, and hung down his back as the fashion was of the last century". There has been some doubt thrown on this description and the only portrait we have of George Kemp hardly bears it out. On the other hand we have the first-hand evidence of George Kemp's own granddaughter who lived all her life in Bournemouth who told a story of how she and her sisters got into most serious trouble with George Kemp on one occasion when, for a prank, they cut off his pigtails as he slept in a chair.

George Kemp was still at the height of his influence, and still the Deacon of the chapel and leader of the Whigs, when in 1834 he suddenly agreed with the mainly Tory objection to the building of the first Poole Bridge. In this he was in direct opposition to most of his party, including his nephew, Martin Kemp Welch who was one of the instigators of the project and also solicitor to the Bridge Company. However, it was he, one Sunday, in company with the Rector of Poole, the Rev Peter Jolliffe, who rushed off to plead with the House of Commons Committee to throw out the Poole Bridge Bill. They feared that drivers of all west-bound traffic would naturally come south through Poole's narrow streets and over the new bridge on their way westward rather than make their horses struggle up Gravel Hill to Wimborne—then the only southern road leading westwards. They feared that if this happened Poole people and its business would suffer.

It was probably this visit as much as the upsurge of the Reform movement which had then been adopted by the Whigs which gave Mr George Lockyer Parrott his opportunity to dislodge George Kemp from the leadership of the Whig/Reform Party in Poole.

James Kemp probably fared better financially than his elder brother George. At least he was able to continue to live in his house in High Street until his death in 1837. Unlike his brother George, he was a supporter of the Poole Corporation against the Reformers' attacks which followed the first and hotly disputed municipal election in Poole. He even signed the Petition to the House of Lords only a few weeks before his death regretting that a Bill had then been brought before Parliament to set aside the Poole election.

George Kemp Senr in his later years amidst the political strife of Poole lost his power to moderate the political storms of the period as the Reformers took over the reins from the old Whigs and turned the party into the Liberal Party. At a meeting in the Guildhall in 1838 George Kemp pleaded with the Party to moderate their fervour and litigious violence, at least so as not seriously to harm the prosperity of Poole. The new leader, George Lockyer Parrott, violently opposed such a quaint notion. Rather than moderate their actions against the 'dishonest' Tory Corporation George Parrott proposed they should "fight the cause in every Court in the Kingdom". The meeting agreed with its new leader and George Kemp's advice was ignored.

In 1811 George Kemp had still owned over 20 houses in Poole as well as his Mansion House, a shop in High Street, cellars and a large store on the Quay at the bottom of High Street and, curiously for a nonconformist, the Bulls Head Inn. The Company of which he was senior partner also owned a dozen or more ocean-going vessels, fishing boats in Newfoundland, stores and a large supply business in Carbonear, Brigus and other places in 1824 when they sold out. Despite this in 1835, he was raising on the mortgage on his Mansion House £2,000 from George

Penney, a fellow Whig, and previously a smaller competitor and, in 1842, there suddenly appeared in Poole a "For Sale" notice, offering the Poole Mansion for £520. In 1843 there was a further sale notice offering 4,500 feet of land for sale at £2,750 plus £100 for the coach house. But none of the property was saleable in the depressed and quarrelling town of Poole before George Kemp's death in June 1845, and he was buried in the Skinner Street chapel, his fortune gone and the town for which he had done so much and for so long was in despair.

Various people lived in the Poole Mansion after George Kemp's death. No doubt Mrs Kemp and her children stayed there for a time and, afterwards Martin Kemp Welch's son, who had the same name as his father, lived there. The families descended from Martin Kemp who died so suddenly in 1772 are very numerous. We can just follow two strands.

George Kemp Junior and his wife on arrival in the USA after a six weeks' journey through a very rough Atlantic both became American citizens within a few months of their arrival in America. They bought a farm at Groveland and built a house there for themselves. It seems therefore, especially as George Kemp Junr described himself as a "Gentleman" in his application for American citizenship, that his father or the business must have provided him and his family well. They had of course, taken with them from Poole their four sons and their daughter who also became American citizens. Their first son, another George Kemp, had been training as a physician before they left Poole but he never practised as a doctor. He and his three brothers, though, all fought in the American Civil War on the Union side. Although they all survived the war, Alfred, born in Poole in 1814, was severely wounded in the head with a sabre at the battle of Gettysburg. Dr George Kemp, the third George, gave his son born in 1867 the same name again, and it was this fourth George Kemp, known as George Ward Kemp, who wrote "The Kemps of Ollantigh and Kemps of Poole" which was published in Seattle in 1939 and which continues the story of many of the Kemps in America.

The only line of the Kemps which continued its active connection with Poole after the death of the two partners of the great firm of G & J Kemp was their youngest brother Martin Kemp who was born just after their father's sudden death in 1772 and who took his uncle's surname of Welch. Martin Kemp Welch had gone into partnership with G W Ledgard in his banks at Poole and Ringwood and was there till his death in 1837. He himself had six sons and a daughter and he called his second son after himself, Martin Kemp Welch. It was this son who became a solicitor and practised in Poole for many years in various partnerships. His first partner was John Durant, the Reform lawyer of Poole.

He married Elizabeth Watts, a relative of Dr Isaac Watts, the famous hymn composer. He was generally credited, together with the agent of the Lord of the Manor, of thinking of and progressing the Bill before Parliament for powers for a private Company to build the first Bridge over Poole Harbour.

Martin Kemp-Welch became the only one of the Kemp family to become

George Kemp II who emigrated to America, 1828.

His wife, Elizabeth Miller Kemp.

Alfred Kemp,
born Poole 1814, son of George Kemp II, in American
Civil War cavalry uniform. Died in Michigan, 1901.

Arthur Kemp,
born Poole 1816, son of George Kemp II, in his American
Civil War officer's uniform (and side view of his cap).
Died in Iowa, 1901.

The Mayor's elegant chair.

involved in the administration of local affairs in Poole. Actually, it was hardly possible for any citizen of any standing in Poole not to get involved in the frenzied Reform days in Poole in the early 19th century, though it did seem that Martin Kemp Welch, having once become involved, showed little anxiety to be free of it.

Even as early as 1838 when the newly-appointed Reform Magistrates immediately dismissed Robert Parr, the old Corporation's Town Clerk, from his post as Clerk to the Magistrates, Martin Kemp Welch was appointed in his place. He held this office for many years afterwards and was never thereafter far from the storm centre of Poole's internecine quarrels. Eventually he became the leader of the Poole liberals and, in 1874, was Mayor, even though by that time he was living in Bournemouth. After he had resigned his position as Magistrate's Clerk, his son, Edward Buckland Kemp-Welch, was appointed in his place, but Edward Kemp Welch died in 1888, only a year after his father, and with his death the Kemp family's immediate connection with Poole was over.

The Kemps had moved eastwards into Christchurch and Bournemouth, into the area from which their ancestors had first come to Poole, though this was almost certainly only coincidental, for in the nineteenth century business in Poole waned sadly and grew in Bournemouth. It was remarkable, however, that Dr James Kemp Welch, Martin's brother, who moved to Christchurch in the mid 1800's to practice as a family doctor there, should take a great interest in the local government of Christchurch and should, like his forebear Thomas Kemp in the 17th century, be chosen by the Christchurch Council to be Mayor of that town three times. It is possible, too, that it was through this connection that the old Mayor's chair of Poole came to get into the chamber of the Christchurch council, for it was Martin Kemp Welch and George W Ledgard who bought the maces and furniture of the Corporation when they were put up to public auction after seizure by the ex-Town Clerk, Robert Parr, on a High Court Writ.

Left in Poole to the memory of the Kemp family is still the Poole Mansion, Creekmoor House and the Kemp Welch School, as well as a fine monument in Poole cemetery to many of the Kemp family. The Poole Mansion after its disposal by the Kemps has had a chequered history.

In 1890 Sir Ivor Guest, the future Lord Wimborne, bought the property and, for the next seven years, Mr Frederick Styring, the owner of the Poole Brewery, who had himself been Mayor of Poole three times, lived there before moving out to the Yarrells at Lytchett Minister.

In 1897, Lord Wimborne offered the house to the Trustees of the Poole Hospital, then occupying Weston House, the old home of the Westons, another old Poole family of merchants, who had built their mansion off a little lane they made from the High Street and which later became known as Weston's Lane. The Poole Mansion then provided accommodation for 30 beds and out-patients' accommodation for the Poole Hospital which was then called "The Cornelia Hospital" after Lady Cornelia Wimborne.

The sale notice for the Poole Mansion House.

For Sale
BY PRIVATE CONTRACT,
THE
HOUSE,
GARDENS, & FIELD,
Late in the occupation of the
Owner, situate in
MARKET STREET
IN POOLE, DORSET.

The LAND, including that on which the
House is built, and comprising the Gardens
and Field, Fence Walls, and other Fences,
and the Trees, at 8d. per foot.

The MANSION HOUSE for £530.
To be taken altogether.

GEORGE KEMP.

Poole, August 1st, 1842.

LANKESTER, PRINTER, HIGH STREET, POOLE.

The Poole Mansion when it was
the Municipal offices and had four letter boxes!

In 1907 the Hospital moved up into Longfleet Road in order to afford the patients the "purer air of Longfleet" as well as to provide for future expansion. The Poole Corporation were then finding the few rooms of the Guildhall quite inadequate for their staff and so took the opportunity to buy the Poole Mansion for use as the Poole Municipal Offices. They paid £1,600 for the building and its immediate curtilage of about an acre of land. The land on the other side of Market Street had been sold separately, its shrubbery and its glorious iron railings, its lake and piped water from the sea had all gone. The Poole Mansion was then used for the next 24 years of its life as Poole's Municipal Offices.

On completion of the present Municipal Offices at Park Gates East in 1932 the Corporation Offices were transferred to the existing building. In moving up to the present offices the Corporation removed the beautiful stained glass window which Sir Peter Thompson had had inserted on the staircase of the Poole Mansion and parts of it were placed as window lights around the Council Chamber. Looking up from the Council Chamber they show up against the sky beautifully in their new position, but the motif of grapes and vines entwining the scenes depicted was lost in the move and the break-up of the window.

The Poole Mansion was afterwards used by the Poole Corporation for educational purposes and many thousands of Poole children and adults have attended day and evening classes there, first under the aegis of the Borough Council and later under the administration of the County Council who rented the premises from the Borough Council.

There was a break in some of the classes in the 1939–45 War when the premises also housed the school medical and dental service. It was here that those children volunteering for evacuation to Canada came for their medical inspection, and it was here that Poole children were joined for their medical and dental care by the Southampton children who shared their schools in wartime.

Now, in 1976, the County Council has relinquished its lease of the premises, and the property has reverted to the Poole Council for a new chapter in the long life of the Poole Mansion to be started.

A Journal of a Voyage
by Gods permission
on board the Brig Mars
David Durell Master

From Greenspond towards the Island Cuivo

by me John B Durell

Chief Mate.

The Journal of the Chief mate of a typical Poole Brig on a voyage which took place
16-24 June, 1834. The trade was then slow: his next voyage was in September,
from London to Cadiz.

Garland

NEC ASPERA TERRENT

W. Tate. 184, Strand.

FAVENTE DEO

Lester

The Mansion House, Thames Street
Stone Cottage, Wimborne
Leeson House, Langton Matravers

For many years the imposing Mansion House in Thames Street was the home of the Lesters, who built it, and of their successors, the Garlands. The history of the Lester family in Poole can be traced back to the 17th century when it appears that John Lester came to settle in the town, possibly from London. While the Newfoundland trade, which was to make the family's fortunes, was at this time comparatively little developed, Poole's other trading interests meant that the town was prosperous enough to attract enterprising merchants and craftsmen from other commercial centres. John Lester was probably a cooper, a skilled craft then much in demand when barrels were used to transport and store all types of goods and the Lesters appear to have specialised as wine coopers first of all.

By the 1690's the Lester family had grown in size and lived in two houses in the High Street. They were clearly prospering and were amongst the few Poole families of the day who employed one man servant and "a mayd". One member of the family had branched out into the butchery business and was renting a house and land at Parkstone from the Lord of Canford Manor, but this side of the family subsequently became quite separate from the Lesters who became merchants in the town. The Lesters were also beginning to play a part in the government of the town; three of them sat on the Corporation and two members of the family served as Mayor in 1716 and 1720. In days when it was not thought necessary to separate the private interests of members of the Corporation from their public concerns, the Lesters' influence in the Corporation helped to forward their business interests. Thus in 1717 when someone complained that Francis Lester and other leading burgesses had enclosed Corporation land to make themselves quays – without permission from the Corporation – not surprisingly the Corporation quickly resolved that this action was not "prejujitial to ye Channel" and should therefore be allowed. Francis Lester however did have to pay a rent of £6 to the Corporation for his new quay, 90 feet long and 54 feet wide.

It was this Francis Lester (1668-1738), a grandson of John Lester, who enlarged the family's business considerably. He married Rachel, the daughter of William Taverner, a substantial Newfoundland merchant who suffered heavy losses in the French attack on St John's Newfoundland in 1709 but was afterwards favoured by the government and appointed to survey the coasts of Newfoundland. This close connection with Newfoundland and the family's business as coopers helped Francis Lester to emerge as a merchant himself, dealing mainly at first in the oil extracted from Newfoundland cod and seals. He owned at least one ship, the *Providence*, which landed "9 tuns of oyle, one puncheon of skins and 1700 deer skins" in Poole in 1731. He was indeed well placed to profit from the recovery in the fisheries which came in the 1720's and with several sons, whom he could hope to train in the trade, could look forward to expanding his business still further.

However, he had to face his share of misfortune in the 1720's. To his horror, his son Francis, who had been sent to work in Lisbon for Charles Lewen, a leading Poole merchant in the Newfoundland trade, decided to renounce his Protestant faith and become a Roman Catholic. (He apparently entered a Jesuit College in Lisbon.) Hostility to Roman Catholicism was particularly strong in Poole; there was a strong dissenting tradition in the community dating back to the days of the Civil War and this had been recently reinforced by the sufferings of the town at the hands of the Catholic King James II and the Catholic Lord of the Manor, Sir John Webb. Francis Lester's despairing letters to Lisbon at this time show how grieved he and his wife were by his son's decision. "He was a lad that lay very near my heart and his mother's, on whom his apostacy has thrown an inexpressible load of grief," he wrote to a business acquaintance in Lisbon in 1724. Despite all of his father's entreaties Francis refused to give up his intentions and disappears from the family records at this time.

Happily, the three brothers of this unfortunate son more than compensated for his loss to the family by their efforts in business and by the time that Francis Lester died in 1738 the family was well entrenched in Poole's economic and social life.

John Lester (1701-75), the eldest son, married well and concentrated on the timber and iron trade from his house and offices in West Street. Importing timber from Scandinavia and North America and iron from Russia, he supplied many of the needs of Poole merchants and shipbuilders, and sent timber to inland towns like Blandford. He played his part too in the affairs of the Corporation and became Mayor in 1744. His period of office was quite eventful for he had to look to the defence of the town in the Jacobite rebellion of 1745 – a rebellion which Poole people took very seriously because of the danger that French forces would land in the area to aid Jacobite sympathisers like the Webb family at Canford. It was decided to dig a defensive ditch across the narrow neck of the peninsula on which the town stood but the cost proved prohibitive and the work was abandoned. Mayor Lester also had the difficult task of paying some of the heavy law debts which the Corporation had recently incurred in their struggles with the Lord of the Manor and at the same time he was faced with increasing complaints from the townspeople about the state of the roads and the quay. Why had the scavenger not carried away "the dirt heaped up on the Great Key"? Why were people allowed to dump "dung and rubbish at the upper end of the High Street so that carriages were obliged to break into the footway causing inconvenience in wet time to passengers on the road walking that way"? There were other alarming traffic problems too: William Preston "Hauled his plough carelessly when passing through the streets, by which means children have often been like to receive damage and likewise he is presented for driving his plough too near people's doors". As if these complaints were not enough, there were as always certain individuals committing various other public nuisances: Mrs Mary Hayter was "continually making use of the Watch House on the Great Key for putting in pitch, tar, etc., that poor distress'd people in storms of rain and wind are debarr'd of shelter," while John Jones and Ruth Lilley were but two of numerous Poole people who kept "scandalous and disorderly houses and entertained vagrants". Even the inmates of the Alms House were at fault for the Quarter Sessions Jury declared that "having received reports of great disorders committed by the inhabitants of the Alms House, we desire that the Overseers would be pleased to examine into their character and behaviour and dismiss some of them". Like other Mayors of his day, John Lester must have been thankful to hand over his office to his successor in 1745; at least he could now relax by indulging in some bathing for in August 1745 the Corporation had agreed that "Mr Mayor at his own expense be allowed to build a house for bathing in the Harbour of Poole on a lease for 21 years at 6d. rent only."

The second of the Lester brothers, Isaac (1718-78), took charge of the family's interest in the Poole end of the Newfoundland trade from a house in Thames Street. Judging by his diaries he was a shrewd, industrious but rather sharp tongued man who did more than hold his own in the ranks of Poole merchants. For example, there was great competition amongst the merchants to secure men for the Newfoundland fisheries and one day Isaac Lester noticed that "John Slade our neighbour is mean enough to ship our people after they have agreed with us, and conceal them. He or his son is at ye door all day and watches to see who goes in or out of our house and nabbes them and gets them into his house." The same day Isaac had his solicitor warn off the offending John Slade. His employees were also treated strictly and if they were drunk or insubordinate might well find themselves "taken up" by the Constable, brought before the Mayor and, like one Thomas Futcher in 1776, clapped into the house of correction to improve their conduct. His diaries are full too of pithy observations about his fellow townsmen: Joshua Mauger, the Poole MP with whom Isaac quarrelled, became "that worthless fellow"; Jack Pike, another merchant, "that scoundrel"; Samuel Bowden, the Mayor, "this ungrateful rascal"; while George Milner, who dared to sympathise with the American rebels, became a "lousy rascal".

Isaac Lester played a leading role in politics in the town but although he served as Sheriff in 1751 did not, as was customary, subsequently become Mayor. This was not for want of trying for he was an unsuccessful candidate on four occasions. At first he may have failed because of his association with John Masters, the ambitious merchant, whose power was then beginning to fade. His later failures may have stemmed from the burgesses' dislike of his sharp tongue. He eventually became nonetheless a power to be reckoned with in both parliamentary and corporation elections. Parliamentary candidates were careful to call at his house to canvass his support and so it was in 1774 that the young Charles James Fox, then a candidate for Poole, "looked in after dinner". From Thames Street Isaac sent messages around

Two rare views of the Lesters' establishment at Trinity, Newfoundland,
painted by an 18th century artist.
In the first, men are engaged in dressing the fish on the fishing stage before it is carried to the
flakes for drying. The larger vessels at anchor wait to take on board the cured fish.

The second view shows Benjamin Lester's house and the warehouses for storing supplies
for his planters and the oil produced from the fish.

Benjamin Lester, MP for Poole 1790–96, Mayor 1781–83.

Benjamin Lester's sister, Sarah, 1710–85.

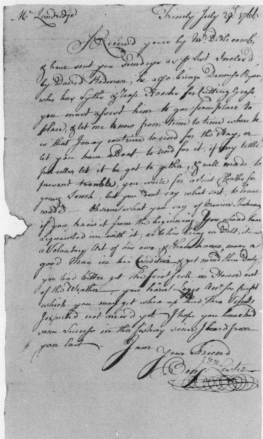

Benjamin Lester sends instructions from Trinity to Joseph Lindridge at Silly Cove.

the town summoning members of the Corporation to his house so that he could check on the latest political and commercial news, make arrangements and give his orders on such matters as the fixing of the poor rate or the election of new burgesses. By the 1770's he was powerful enough to secure the election of Mayors of his own choice who were then frequently called to Thames Street to receive his commands.

This growing political influence in Poole rested on an increasingly large share of the Newfoundland trade and Isaac's careful management of business in Poole was matched by the enterprise and industry of his younger brother Benjamin (1724-1802) who worked for many years in Newfoundland itself. Benjamin Lester had gone there as a youth about 1740 and had first served as an agent for John Masters, a Newfoundland merchant from Poole, and his Irish partner Michael Ballard. He strengthened his opportunities to develop trade there on his own account by marrying in Trinity, Newfoundland, his cousin, the daughter of another Newfoundland merchant, Jacob Taverner, a Poole family established very early in Trinity. Lester came to supervise a large trading empire extending over Fogo Island, Bonavista and Trinity Bays in the north of the island from a headquarters in Trinity. He is said to have been only the second merchant to settle there and in 1760 built himself a large brick house, then one of the comparatively few buildings in the island not constructed from wood and now the oldest building standing in Newfoundland. From here he controlled the fisheries in the out-stations like Silly Cove, Old Perlican and Catalina in Trinity Bay and Greenspond in Bonavista Bay, sending supplies and instructions to his planters and servants, such as Joseph Lindridge in Silly Cove. From Trinity too he dispatched the vessels of the Lester fleet carrying mainly oil, skins and furs to Poole, and cod fish to Portugal, Spain, Italy and the West Indies. By the 1770's this fleet comprised at least twelve ships which have been identified by name – the *Amy, Betsey, Fame, Industrious Bee, John, Joseph and Benjamin, Mary, Sally, Susan, Thomas, Two Brothers* and the *Two Sisters*. They were not always sufficient for the needs of the Lesters' growing trade and on occasions other merchant's ships were chartered to carry cargoes for them: for example, in 1776 Christopher Jolliffe's brig *Sukey* took a cargo of fish from Trinity to Jamaica for the Lesters.

Benjamin Lester's own account of his time in Newfoundland shows how life and work in the island was generally hard and frequently dangerous. The people in Trinity were more fortunate than those in smaller settlements in that they had a doctor, but his services were of a dubious quality. When, for example, he arrived to treat Lester for an injury caused by a fall on the ice, Benjamin noted that he was "drunk as usual". Shortages of essential provisions and supplies for the fisheries were a continual source of worry for the merchants and planters. In 1768 the *Two Brothers* failed to arrive from Spain with a cargo of salt and Lester confided in his diary, "I fear they are all miscarry'd and . . . leaves us the great loss of the Poor Souls on board and in great want of salt". Sudden storms in Newfoundland waters also caused loss of life and supplies as in 1767 when, "Mr Porter, Mate of the *Bee*, went away with six hands for Tilting Harbour to haul bait, hasn't been heard of since, fear they are all lost". His fears were correct for the wreck of the boat was subsequently found off Bonaventura. It is no wonder that those working in such arduous conditions sought some consolation in rum and other strong drink. Twice a day each workman in Trinity expected not tea or coffee but a drink of rum and a piece of hard biscuit, while occasions like weddings were celebrated in veritable floods of liquor. Supplies of rum were readily available from ships returning from the West Indies while other liquors were imported from Britain. Sometimes these came from smugglers' stocks. For example, once when Lester was returning to Newfoundland on the *Betsey* and was delayed in Poole Harbour, he went ashore at North Haven, (Sandbanks), one of the smugglers' resorts, and bought a keg of brandy for 36 shillings.

Lester demonstrated his enterprise in Newfoundland by using new methods in the seal fisheries. According to A C Wardle, in 1778 he began to use shallops, light open boats, to search out the seals in the springtime, instead of relying on the rather haphazard methods of fishing from the shore which had been used hitherto. He was rewarded with much greater catches in Ragged Harbour and Dog Bay and one of his vessels is reported later coming into Poole with as many as 6,000 skins and 107 tons of oil on board. Between fishing seasons there were opportunities to use his employees and the ready supplies of local timber to build boats. Many of these were naturally small craft, like the shallops for the seal fisheries, but some were larger vessels like the Lesters' brig *Bonavista* which was built to take part in the Newfoundland banks fishery but was also pressed into service to carry cargoes to Europe. Benjamin also undertook the construction of ships for the Royal Navy.

He was in Newfoundland during the Seven Years War (1756-63) when one of the principal objects of rivalry between Britain and France was control over the island's fisheries. In fact peace negotiations, which began in 1761 and could have made the war the "Five Years War" instead, broke down partly over the question of Newfoundland because William Pitt, the British war leader, refused to listen to the French foreign minister when he said, "Give us some of the fishing and we will make peace". Having failed to persuade the British by diplomatic means, the French turned their forces on Newfoundland in 1762 and gave the merchants there, and back in Britain, their greatest fright since the early years of the century.

In June 1762 the French made a strong attack on Newfoundland, capturing St John's, the principal settlement, as well as smaller settlements such as Carbonear, Ferryland and Bonavista. Some of the merchants and planters lost heavily; for example John Pike and his clerk, John Bowles – both from Poole – were captured in Carbonear. Bowles was carried back to France and Pike lost his "papers, boats, cloaths and furr" but escaped the fate of his clerk when Admiral Lord Colville's fleet arrived to drive off the French. "What an uncivilised and barbarous manner of making war is this? How different from our behaviour at Guadeloupe and Martinique!" he protested. Trinity too was captured by the French but Benjamin Lester is said to have behaved with such clever diplomacy that he and the other merchants there escaped virtually unscathed.

According to the late Walter White's History of Trinity, Benjamin Lester realised that it would be pointless to resist the French and accordingly when the invasion force under Admiral de Terney dropped anchor in the harbour, he immediately sent the Admiral a polite invitation to dinner. Surprised by this gesture, the Admiral accepted and was greeted by Lester on the wharf. "At the Lester house that night wines and spirits flowed like water; the fattest chickens were served and everything went merry, and joy was unconfined." When the Admiral had eaten and drunk his fill Benjamin was able to secure his promise that the Lester's property would not be destroyed. Benjamin was to send a man who would accompany the French raiders to point out the Lester property, which was to be left alone. The man was duly coached by Lester and on the following day the French began to row around the harbour to carry out the destruction of the boats and shore installations. As they went, "the French Lieutenant asked, 'Whose property is this?' 'It's Mr Lester's', and 'Whose property is this?' 'That's Mr Lester's', and so they continued until the Lieutenant became impatient and said, 'Why d––n it, it's all Mr Lester's,' and throughout the whole day, the only devestation was the burning of one new vessel which was on the stocks, and about half finished."

As might be expected, the story of this episode has gained something from re-telling over the passage of time since 1762 and the truth about what happened in Trinity is a little more prosaic, although it bears out some of the traditional account. Benjamin Lester's own description of the events shows that there was much more destruction: the fort and many of the fishing stages and boats were destroyed and the French took much of the inhabitants' stocks of provisions. Nevertheless, the amount of destruction was limited, partly because of the advance warning of the French attack received by the people in Trinity and partly because of Benjamin Lester's wise leadership. When news came that St John's had surrendered to the French without firing a shot, the merchants and sea captains were able to save the 18 ships then in Trinity by moving them into another harbour or, as with Lester's brig the *John*, sailing them to Britain. Lester then sensibly persuaded some of the inhabitants who wanted to make a fight for the port that they were so out gunned that resistance would only bring greater destruction and loss. Thus when the French squadron arrived at Trinity, each side fired one token shot and having satisfied honour, the English then hauled down their colours. As the senior magistrate in Trinity, Lester subsequently used great tact in dealing with the invaders and by satisfying their demands for provisions was able to limit the amount of destruction. By clever negotiations with the French he also managed to secure their agreement that most of the fishing stages should be pulled down, rather than burnt. This made it possible to save the fish and oil, reduced the danger that fire would spread to houses and stores and also made easier the task of rebuilding. Similarly he was able to arrange that the half-built ship he had on the stocks should be cut up instead of burnt. Lester certainly tried hard to entertain the French commander to dinner, with a view to further reducing the settlement's losses, but

Fillets of dried cod fish in marble on the fireplace of the dining room in the
Thames Street Mansion House.

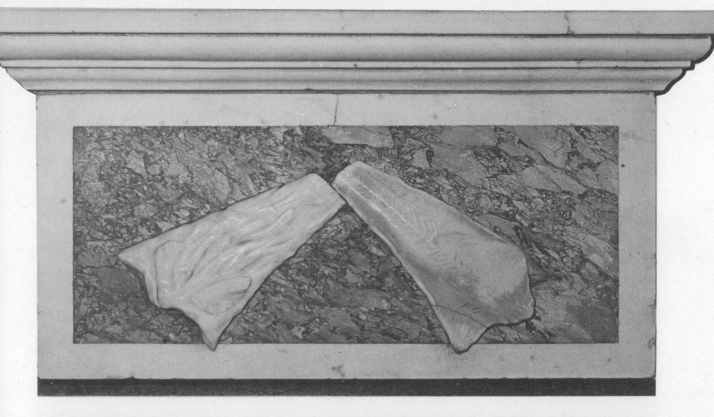

Personal mementoes of the Lester and Garland families:
Benjamin Lester's spectacles and spectacle case, Isaac Lester's notebook, buttons from
Sir John Lester's coat and the gorget of the Rev Lester Lester when he was an officer in the
11th Hussars.

he refused these repeated invitations. However, Lester was able to establish reasonably friendly relations with the French who on one occasion displayed their traditional gallantry by returning to Mrs Lester a particularly fine cow which they had taken from Lester's herd. They also entertained Benjamin Lester to dinner on board one of their vessels. He remarked afterwards that "our dinner was a variety of dishes but not to my liking", and probably regarded this meal as a further sacrifice he had made for the sake of his fellow inhabitants! As a result of Lester's diplomacy the people of Trinity were able to begin the task of repairing their property as soon as the French left on 1st August 1762. The 16 days of enemy occupation could have been a much more terrifying and costly experience.

Lester's calm reaction contrasted very strongly with that of the planters elsewhere, where vain attempts were made to resist the French and the settlements were destroyed. It contrasted too, with the panic that spread through Poole when Captain Hewlett of Lester's brig *John* sailed in to the port bringing the news of the French attack. "This news throws this town and the country around us into the deepest consternation", wrote the Poole correspondent of a local newspaper, and the Newfoundland merchants in the town immediately stopped business. However, it was not long before the French were driven off and the peace treaty of 1763 confirmed the advantages which the English merchants had gained over the French fisheries in Newfoundland. Although this treaty did not satisfy the most aggressive of the merchants, it provided some consolation for losses during the war. The Poole merchants also made an attempt to secure compensation for those who had suffered in the 1762 invasion of Newfoundland by a petition to Parliament but this was thrown out when it was noticed that all the signatures were in the same hand!

While his brother was busy in Newfoundland, Isaac Lester, like many Poole merchants, was determined to invest some of the family's profits in property: in 1766 he started building a house at Lytchett Minster and developed a farm there. This house, Post Green, was a convenient country retreat from a crowded Poole, while the produce of the farm was useful as a contribution to food supplies for Newfoundland – finding sufficient foodstuffs in the Poole area became an increasingly serious problem for the merchants of the town as the fisheries prospered. Isaac was however principally concerned to obtain a better house in Poole itself to replace what he described in his letters as "this old hut". At last in 1776 he was able to achieve his aim. Having acquired the house next door to his existing house in Thames Street, he commissioned a Poole builder, John Swetland, to pull it down and replace it with a much grander building. This was the Mansion House which Benjamin Lester was later to complete with an additional storey and other embellishments, including the elegant marble fireplace depicting the dried cod which was the origin of the family's fortunes. Isaac Lester's anxieties over the house did not end with the start of the building operations for he soon found himself accused by the Quarter Sessions Jury of allowing the building to encroach on public property. Characteristically, but probably with much justice, Isaac blamed two of his rivals in the town for raising the matter – "that villiain Hyde and John Slade who was foreman of the jury". He had little need to worry however; the Mayor was promptly summoned to Thames Street and since he owed his election to Isaac, very readily agreed that the jury had behaved improperly. A small alteration to the pavement outside the house ended the dispute.

Isaac Lester did not live to see the completion of the house he had so longed for because he died in 1778. Benjamin Lester, who had finally returned from Newfoundland in 1770, leaving the business there in the charge of Thomas Stone, now took over the family's business and political power in the town. He was a more tolerant man than his brother: there are far fewer "rascals" and "scoundrels" in his papers, and he enjoyed playing cards at "ye Club at ye Old Antelope" or entertaining the Aldermen to "coffy". He was more generous too to St James Church and although he did not always see eye to eye with the Rectors, presented an organ to the Church in 1799. At its installation he was pleased to note that there was "a Cathedral service much approved by all hands".

Benjamin was also a man of wider interests and more far-reaching ambitions. He soon set about increasing his family's power in the town, making himself Mayor for three years and involving himself very closely with Joseph Gulston, one of the borough's MPs. Eventually, after Gulston had lost his seat, partly through his own feckless attitude, Benjamin put himself forward as a candidate and was returned to the Commons at his first attempt in 1790.

Long before his election to Parliament Benjamin Lester had become thoroughly familiar with the ways of Ministers and Members of Parliament. Together with his brother Isaac, he had been a close supporter of two of the MPs for Poole in the 1760's and '70's, Joshua Mauger and General Sir Eyre Coote, and through them he had become known to Lord North, the Prime Minister 1770-82, and Earl Sandwich, for long the First Lord of the Admiralty. Indeed, in 1775 Benjamin Lester found himself addressing the House of Commons and the Lords and playing a part in bringing on the American Revolution which was to make the American rebels identify him as one of their principal enemies.

By the year 1775 the British government had grown tired of what they regarded as the unreasonable attitude of the American colonists and their rebellious conduct in such episodes as the notorious Boston Tea Party. They were determined to teach their unruly North American subjects a lesson and planned several punitive measures. Amongst these was a "bill to restrain the Trade and Commerce of the Provinces of Massachusett's Bay and New Hampshire and Colonies of Connecticut and Rhode Island and Providence Plantation . . . and to prohibit such Provinces and Colonies from carrying on any Fishery on the Banks of Newfoundland. . . ." This the Government hoped would hurt the colonists in their pockets, and perhaps their stomachs, and so bring them to their senses. However, opinion in Britain on this policy was bitterly divided; the majority undoubtedly supported it, agreeing with the King and his Ministers that it was the time to check the ill behaved colonists but a substantial minority in the country opposed the

LONDON.

PUBLIC LEDGER, March 15, 1775.

IT has been difcovered that the petition from the Corporation of Poole, againft the people of New England, was conceived at the ADMIRALTY, and brought forth in PARLIAMENT-Street, and that in order to get the fame acknowledged by its reputed parents, a noble Lord at the Treafury was obliged to make an abfolute promife, that the FEES which are at prefent paid on all fhips at Newfoundland, fhould be DISCONTINUED, and that he would intereft himfelf to procure a decifion in the Houfe of Commons in favour of the exclufive right of the Corporation to elect Members of Parliament; this, it feems, one of the witneffes, out of the fullnefs of his heart, with the affiftance of a little wine, could not help divulging by way of triumph.

CONTROVERTED ELECTION.

Public Ledger, and Gazetteer. Monday 27, of March 1775.

On Saturday the Committee appointed to try the merits of the POOLE Election, met at Ten o'clock.

PETITIONERS.	SITTING MEMBERS.
Hon. C. J. Fox, and	Sir E. Coote, K. B. and
John Williams, Efq;	Jof. Mauger, Efq;

CHAIRMAN.
LORD CHARLES SPENCER.

NOMINEES.

Lord Lifburne.	Mr. Adam.
George Grenville Efq;	Sir John Eden.
Hon. Mr. Carey	Sir Adam Fergufon.
Mr. Powys	Mr. Elwes.
Charles Turner Efq;	Tho. Freeman Efq;
James Worfley Efq;	T. Knight Efq;
Sir William Guife	J. Tempeft Efq;

COUNCIL.

Elliot and Allen.	Wilfon and Batt.

The Petitioners Council opened the bufinefs, when Lord Lifburne defired to know " what was the laft determination of the Houfe?' " It was read, and appears as follows: " In 1618 an Election for POOLE came on before a committee of the Houfe of Com- " mons, when they reported, that by antient ufage the right of voting lay in the Mayor, " Bailiffs, and Burgeffes, but by an Act of the 18 James the Firft, the right lay in the " Mayor, Bailiffs, Burgeffes, and COMMONALTY, and accordingly they decided " it in favour of the latter cuftom, '" When the report of the Committee was made " to the Houfe, and the queftion put that the Houfe fhould agree with the Committee, " a NEGATIVE was put upon it, but for what reafon could not be found out."

The Council on BOTH fides contended, that it was in their favour, and according-ly put different conftructions on the negative.

The Committee ordered the room to be cleared, and after about an hour's deliberation, the Council were call'd in and informed, they might go on to PROVE the antient cuftom.

Mr. ALLEN accordingly read abftracts from the different Charters that had been granted to POOLE. The firft was that granted in the reign of Richard the firft, by Richard Long-fword, natural fon of Henry the 2d; that was confirmed in 1372, by Edward the Third. The next confirmation was by Thomas de Montague, in 1411. The next, which was the firft Royal Charter, was by Henry the Sixth, in 1423, which made POOLE a free port. In the 31ft of Henry the Sixth, 1443, a charter was granted, INCORPORATING all the inhabi-tants. In the 1ft of Edward the Fourth, a confirmation of thofe rights was granted. In the 3d of Henry the Eighth, 1512, a farther confirmation was granted; and in the 12th of the fame King a ftill farther confirmation paffed. The next was a charter, confirming all the former, by Arthur Plantagenet, Lord High Admiral of Eng-land, which fays, " The Corporation SHALL confift of " Mayor, Bailiffs, Burgeffes, and INHABITANTS. The next was that of Le Clarencieux, King at Arms, who infpected into their Arms, and confirmed their Charter. The 10th of Elizabeth runs thus, " The Mayor, Bailiffs, Burgeffes, and INHABITANTS, fhall enjoy " all Corporate rights' " and in another claufe the Charter declares that " the Burgeffes and inhabitants fhall be a Corporation," under the above title. In the 18th of James the Firft, " Mayor, Aldermen, and COM-MONALTY, was the form. In 1658, continued the Council, the Corporation wanted to ftrike off the COM-MONALTY, and in the year 1661 we fee the Commonalty left out, and for the firft time in 1695.

The 7th of William, the Mayor, Aldermen, Burgeffes, & COMMONALTY, were incorporated; fome of the inhabitants figned Burgeffes, others did not. On 15th of September 1570, a Sheriff was elected out of the COM-MONALTY, another the 14th of April 1592. The 3d of November 1645, the Corporation was convened, and a bye-law made, which erafed the word COMMONALTY, and inferted that of INHABITANTS.

In 1668, the COMMONALTY chofe a Recorder. In the 33d of Edward the Sixth, the inhabitants returned MEMBERS. He mentioned a Cafe which happened at Dover, where formerly the right of voting lay in all the Barons, but in the 3d of Elizabeth, the Mayor and JURATS made a bye-law, and vefted the right of elec-tion in a few; the affair was brought before the Houfe of Commons, and they determined, " that no ufage or Bye-law could take away a Man's RIGHT." The original Charters were then delivered in, and from the Antiquity of them, they took up the remainder of the Day reading.

The Public Ledger newspaper attacks Poole Corporation's petition against the American colonists and alleges collusion between the Government and the Corporation over the Poole election dispute.

measures. Many merchants, especially those of the City of London, argued that the Government's plans would only goad the Americans into more desperate conduct and in any case would prevent them from paying the very large debts they owed to British merchants. There was too a growing number of radicals in Britain who sympathised with the belief of some Americans that George III and Parliament were behaving in a tyrannical manner. Opinion in Poole was likewise divided. The majority of the merchants were naturally disposed to support the King and his Ministers against his rebellious subjects and amongst them some, including the Lesters, saw advantages for their trade in a ban on the colonists' fisheries: they argued that they would be able to take over the Americans' trade with the West Indies. Other Poole merchants were not sure that this would be a worthwhile extension to their trade and were afraid that cutting off food supplies from North America to Newfoundland would ruin the fisheries.

The situation in Poole in 1775 was further complicated by the existence of a few radicals who were already in dispute with the Corporation and now took up the American question as well. The dispute with the Corporation concerned the right to vote in parliamentary elections and had flared up in the General Election of 1774. The Corporation argued that they alone had the right to vote while the radicals and their supporters, maintained that the Borough's charter entitled all householders to vote. The radicals, or the Commonalty as they were called, had disputed the result of the 1774 election and the whole issue was before the House of Commons early in 1775. Many members of the Corporation were afraid that if they showed themselves hostile or only lukewarm towards the Government's policy towards the Americans there was a grave danger that the Ministers would not support their claim to keep their exclusive right to the vote. Naturally enough some supporters of the Commonalty had come out in support of the American colonists and feelings in the town ran very high with accusations of tyranny and disloyalty being freely exchanged. One of the radicals apparently went so far as to say that he hoped that the Americans would cut the throats of the troops sent to put them down and wished "that the heads of those that sent them were on Temple Bar".

In face of this threat to the power of the Corporation, dominated as it was by merchants, and horrified by the treasonous talk of the radicals, the Lesters and a majority of the Burgesses were determined to come out in public support of the Government's policy. They accordingly adopted a loyal address to the King praising the plan to cut off the trade of the colonists. This was a god-send to Lord North whose policy was under heavy attack from his opponents and he made sure that it was quickly presented to George III and publicised in the press. The Prime Minister decided too to make use of the loyalty of the Poole merchants to help steer the American trade and fisheries bill through Parliament: Benjamin Lester with all his experience in Newfoundland was the ideal witness to use and thus on 6th March 1775 he was "examined" before the Committee of the Whole House and nine days later as "a merchant adventurer for 38 years", gave evidence before the House of Lords. He spoke at some length, arguing that no harm would come to the fisheries because the British merchants could fill any gaps created by the ban on the Americans taking part in the fisheries or supplying provisions to Newfoundland. Moreover, the value of Newfoundland as "a nursery of seamen" would be much increased if the Americans were excluded because it had never proved possible to enforce on them the regulations regarding the employment of "landsmen" in the fisheries (and thus provide training for seamen who could be used in time of war).

After a month's debate the Goverment was able to pass its measures and shortly afterwards the House of Commons Committee investigating the Poole election dispute upheld the exclusive right of the members of the Corporation to the vote. The Corporation were overjoyed at their victory over what one of them called "the deluded multitude" but the Commonalty were enraged and proclaimed that the Corporation had only preserved their unjust privilege by agreeing with the Government to "butcher and starve their American brethren". In fact some people did starve; they were not the American colonists but many of the unfortunate inhabitants of Newfoundland who could no longer obtain food supplies from the Americans and found that the British merchants could not make up the shortage for two years. As for the American colonists, their determination to resist the British Government was greatly hardened and meeting together in their first Congress they all agreed to prohibit trade of any sort with Britain. They began to arm themselves and in April 1775 Paul Revere made his famous ride to rouse the rebel forces against the British troops in Massachusetts. The path to the Revolution was open and the merchants of Poole, out of a mixture of loyalty and self-interest, had in a small but significant way helped to widen this path.

Benjamin Lester naturally very much regretted the Americans' achievement of their independence in 1783, preceded as it had been by the downfall of Lord North, after whom he had loyally named one of his ships. However, he continued to be involved with Ministers and their aides, and in 1785 was called before the Privy Council to give evidence on the American trade question. He was then able to help persuade the Government to permit imports of American provisions into Newfoundland only if they were carried in British ships. Only very gradually did the hositility of Poole merchants towards the independent Americans begin to wane as they realised that American supplies were becoming essential to the fisheries.

After an apprenticeship of this nature in national politics, winning the Poole election in 1790 was a comparatively straight forward task for him. Nonetheless, he displayed great care and real talent in using the then customary methods of electioneering. As he once wrote, "I tickled the people according to the laws of the country and some I also tickled according to the laws of Election – *you know what those laws are*!" This method of "tickling" the electors sometimes involved direct cash payments or very often promises of favours from Government – a job or a contract. In any case the voters would expect small presents and Benjamin Lester was careful to distribute amongst them gifts of fish and cranberries (a delicacy then obtained from Newfoundland). More important men warranted rather larger presents; for example he presented Lord Shaftesbury with a 57 lb cod fish (which cost only 3d.). The electors also expected some entertainment: Benjamin's son had the local theatre put on a play for the burgesses and their wives, who also enjoyed themselves at the election night ball, which cost Lester £371 – "to my great surprise". The common people, although without votes, also had to be remembered for they provided the election mobs which intimidated opponents with their jeers and worse, and heartened the candidate and his supporters with their cheers. Lester thus had to find the money for distributing a large quantity of bread and beef to the poor on Christmas Eve 1789 and beer and ribbons during the actual election. Fighting a successful election also required rather more subtle manoeuvres – a watch had to be kept on the opposition who would try any means, including a form of kidnapping, to prevent hostile electors from voting. This happened in 1790 when "one of our voters, young Richard Linthorne, went off, with some of our enemies, carried out of Town . . . we are much hurt by it". Naturally the weaker willed voters had to be protected against interference and Benjamin Lester "set Captain Dawe to work packing goods to keep him out of temptation as his wife is constantly plaguing him to receive money" (for his vote).

His election to Parliament, where he sat until 1796, meant fresh responsibilities and new honours. The new member had to satisfy the needs of his constituents for places and favours from Government and Lester was kept busy arranging for young Linthorne to become a tide-waiter (a clerk) in the Customs Service, while more senior men like Edward Allen and John Strong had to be fitted in to higher posts. When war broke out with France in 1793 the merchants of the town naturally looked to their MPs to assist in arranging convoys for their ships and to protect their seamen from the incursions of the press gang as far as possible. Benjamin Lester had begun to move into county society even before his election to the Commons. Back in 1785 he had been invited to the wedding between Sir John Webb's daughter and the Earl of Shaftesbury and had noted in his diary that "His Lordship behaved very politely and took me by ye arm sometimes". Well might Lord Shaftesbury behave so politely for Lester's wealth was such that he was accustomed to lending money to at least one member of the aristocracy. Now as an MP, Lester became a County Magistrate and in 1796 was appointed a Deputy Lieutenant of the County with the responsibility for the defence of Poole. (Both his son-in-law and his grandson were commissioned in the volunteer forces raised in Poole and Dorset to resist the threatened French invasion.)

Quite apart from his public duties he had of course to continue his careful supervision of his business. By the 1780's he was converting catches of nearly 400,000 fish into about 10,000 quintals of dried cod with 87 men working on the Newfoundland banks and needed more wharves in Poole for his trade. He began to build two large quays at the rear of his premises in West Street, which were used mainly for imports of timber. Material to reclaim land for these quays was obtained from Horse Island in the harbour, an island which in the end disappeared because it was so often used for this purpose. He also had to extend his quay at the back of the

Mansion House in Thames Street to help accommodate his growing fleet of ships. By 1793 these numbered approximately 30 vessels and constituted one of the largest, if not the largest fleet belonging to a Poole merchant. Those that have been identified by name were: the brigs *Mercury, John, Fame, Swallow, Labrador* and *Little Ben*; the brigantine *Betsey*, and the snow *Ceres*. Other vessels were: *The Victory, Industry, Hope, Amy, Cabot, Industrious Bee, Maria, Bingley, Susan, Lord North, Catherine, Fly, Joseph and Francis, Caractacus, Providence*, and the *Horse Shoe Club*.

A typical cargo brought into Poole on one of these ships at this time included the following items:

6 tons of Train Oil

99 tons of Seal Oil

9 tons of Seal Blubber

6,596 Seal Skins

12 Cow Hides

24 Calf Hides

2 Bear Skins

298 Beaver Skins

200 Otter Skins

2 White Fox Skins

18 Yellow Fox Skins

12 Silver Fox Skins

60 Boards, 1,000 feet

300 Small Poles

2 Bundles of Old Nets

7–28 lb Bags of Coffee

1 Barrel of Fish

1 Watch to be repaired.

Some of his ships became casualties in the war against France which began in 1793. For example the *Susan* was seized by a French privateer while actually in convoy and the crew were imprisoned in Nantes. The *Joseph and Francis* had the misfortune to be taken and plundered by the French and, when subsequently recovered by the Royal Navy, was plundered a second time by British sailors at Guernsey. Both the *John* and the *Industrious Bee* were captured by the French and then retaken by the Navy, although only the mate remained free from the crew of the *John*. Other ships had lucky escapes – the *Lord North* just managed to reach Lisbon with a Spanish privateer in headlong pursuit of her, while a later addition to the fleet, the *Halifax*, was so badly damaged in a storm in the Atlantic that a privateer which came up with her took pity on her and let her go free. Replacements for these losses and other additions to the Lester fleet were either built in Newfoundland or bought from other British ports because Benjamin Lester seems to have had a low opinion of Poole ship builders like Meadus and Burt. The latter once offered to build a 278 ton ship for Lester for £5,050, "a monstrous price" Benjamin noted in his diary.

The view of Upton House as one approaches the main entrance.

The main entrance hall and staircases of Upton House.

The rear of Upton House; the garden extends to the edge of Holes Bay.

The front elevation of the Poole Mansion in the late 19th century.

The Poole Mansion, Sir Peter Thompson's house in Market Close, from an early colour print

The Mansion House, Thames Street, Poole, now the premises of the Mansion House Club.

Stone Cottage, Wimborne Minster, now known as Stone Park.

Leeson House, Langton Matravers, Dorset.

A mantelpiece in Leeson House showing the clever use of carved woodwork from Flanders.

Post Green, Lytchett Minster. The Lesters reputedly used this house as a place to hide their seamen from the Press Gang. On Benjamin Lester's death, Post Green passed to his daughter, Sarah Pointer, and subsequently to the Lees family.
It is now the home of Sir Thomas and Lady Lees who have made it the centre for the Post Green Christian Community.

Fiddleford Mill, the home of "olde Thomas Whyghtt, a great ryche marchantt".

Beech Hurst in the mid-nineteenth century, still shaded by trees.

Beech Hurst, High Street, Poole.

The Rectory, with the original iron railings still enclosing the front garden.

The war brought other problems for Lester and the other merchants. Insurance rates increased alarmingly and the press gang moved further afield to capture men for Naval service. By 1793 the press gang was not only ignoring "protections" issued by the Mayor of Poole for men who were pilots for the port but was searching out likely men in Wimborne. They were active too in Newfoundland. Finding willing hands for Poole ships thus became an even greater problem than usual and those who were recruited often had to be allowed to fortify their courage with liquor before they would undertake voyages made more perilous than usual by the dangers of war time. On one occasion, having spent much time finding enough bread for one of his vessels to carry to Newfoundland and delayed her sailing, Lester was disgusted to find that the crew were all drunk. They "promis'd to be on board in ye morning and to sail from ye wharf. Wish that it may be the case, but I fear it." He was right to be doubtful for an adverse wind and the crew's befuddled heads meant that the ship did not succeed in negotiating its way out of the harbour until 4 o'clock the following afternoon. Sometimes too members of the crew were left behind when their ships sailed and in 1800 Lester "with great trouble hired a sloop to put on board . . . that scoundrell Anthony Barrow" who had missed his ship. (Men were so difficult to recruit that it was evidently worth going to this expense.) There were of course a few compensations for Poole merchants during the war – mainly in the form of Government contracts. Lester's ship *Halifax* was used to carry supplies to Halifax, Nova Scotia, for the troops there.

War-time Poole presented other problems to Lester and his fellow magistrates who included his son John (Mayor from 1789 to 1795). The population of the town was swollen by numerous regiments of the army and the militia, some standing by to defend the coast against possible French invasion and some awaiting transport to theatres of war overseas, such as the West Indies. They and their camp followers placed a great strain on the accommodation and primitive sanitary arrangements then available. The Quarter Sessions juries waxed indignant over the way in which the soldiers deposited their rubbish around the barracks near Hunger Hill and were "putting excrement in the lane running from Strand Street to the King's Arms". Even the pavements in the High Street were obstructed by sentry mounts. "Disorderly houses" such as William Hewlett's "Crown and Thistle" did a roaring trade and it was presumably the relaxation of normal standard of decency which caused Mr Levy to exhibit "an obscene Sign over his door on the Quay, the same being indecent". Food supplies were a problem too. In 1800 "a mob of men and women assembled in the market and demanded setting a price on meat and butter. The Justices read the Riot Act and dispersed them, putting some in gaol, one woman in particular who was at ye head, a vile creature, her maiden name Hart." It is not surprising that it was during the war that the Poole magistrates at length decided to build a new gaol for the town. There had been many complaints about the inadequacy of the old one in Fish Street; in 1788 it was said that it was "not only in a ruinous condition but highly inconvenient to the trades of this town by obstructing the passage of carriages to and from the Quays". The new gaol in King Street

George Garland, MP for Poole 1801–06, Mayor 1788 and 1810.

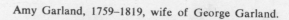
Amy Garland, 1759–1819, wife of George Garland.

Sir John Lester, 1754–1805, Mayor of Poole 1789–95.

Benjamin Lester Lester, 1779–1838, MP for Poole 1809–35, Mayor 1815.

provided more secure and wholesome accommodation for its inmates and made it possible to pull down the old one and widen Fish Street.

From all these cares Benjamin Lester could obtain some rest and relaxation out at his substantial "cottage" and farm at Stanley Green, then a peaceful rural area outside Poole. Here he could enjoy "tea and syllabub" on hot afternoons or watch the antics of his pet bear, but even domestic life was troubled on occasions. In 1791 he "put another collar on the Bare's Neck by which he is much displeased," and the bear in fact died shortly afterwards! On a more serious note, one of his young granddaughters would not learn or pay attention to her governess and Benjamin, no doubt with mock fierceness, threatened "to put her in the workhouse, which had some effect and she promis'd to learn better". Servants too could be troublesome: early in 1800 his cook got so drunk that he was forced to put her in the House of Correction. Next day she was dismissed with a month's wages and a lecture and replaced by "a cook-maid, £6 6s. 0d. a year, to find her own tea and be on tryal for a month".

A more serious problem arose from the fact that Benjamin had only two sons, of whom one only lived to manhood. Since this son, John, did not enjoy good health, and his children did not survive, there was great danger that the formidable business empire he had done so much to build would eventually be broken up like those of other successful merchants without adequate heirs. Fortunately Benjamin found a talented assistant in George Garland, who became one of his family when he married Benjamin's daughter Amy in 1779. George Garland (1753-1825) was the son of a substantial yeoman farmer of East Chaldon who had as a boy played with the children of the Weld family at Lulworth Castle. With his elder brother, Joseph, he had come to Poole and set up a business in the corn trade. In this way he came to know the Lesters who needed large supplies of bread for supplying the Newfoundland fisheries but because Garland had to travel widely in Europe to negotiate purchases of corn, he often had to carry on a long distance courtship with Amy. He has left us amongst his papers one of his poems to Amy, written in far away Prussia. To "her bright eyes" he wrote:

"Blest be the lovely fair whose gentle hands
Bids her thoughts boldly brave a foreign land,
And kindly hastens with a trembling quill
Softly to say, I love and always will . . ."

Their marriage fulfilled the promise of this verse in its happiness; they had eleven children, eight of them sons, the eldest of whom was naturally called Benjamin Lester after his distinguished grandfather. By his will Benjamin Lester arranged that much of his property in Poole should pass to this grandson Benjamin on the death of his own son, provided that his grandson took the surname of Lester. His son-in-law, George Garland, was to inherit the Newfoundland business. In his later years then Benjamin Lester was sure that the great business house of Lester would continue in the hands of the family and that his name would also be preserved.

Benjamin died in January 1802, busy to the end in the affairs of Poole and his business. His last work in Poole was to settle with the magistrates the amount of the award to be made to those who had salvaged goods from a shipwreck nearby, while just three days before his death, he noted with satisfaction in his diary that his ship the *Lord North* had left Trinity for Poole with a cargo of blubber and oil. St James Church benefited from his will because he left £400 to the Corporation to pay the organist there a salary of £20 per annum for ever. Unfortunately however, Benjamin Lester did not live quite long enough to see his son knighted by George III in June 1802 when he presented a loyal address to the King on the conclusion of peace with France.

Sir John Lester himself did not survive long to enjoy his new status for he died at Bath, where he had gone for the sake of his health, early in 1805. He too remembered St James Church in his will and left over £2,500 to the Rector so that an evening service and sermon could be held each Sunday, thus providing for a long felt need in the town. (Should the Rector omit to hold the service or preach his sermon £1 was to be deducted from the sum for each neglect of his duty.) Later in 1805 Benjamin Lester Garland, in accordance with his grandfather's will and "out of grateful and affectionate respect" for him, obtained a Royal license to change his name and became Benjamin Lester Lester.

In many ways George Garland who now became the head of the family and its extensive business interests reinforced the strength of the Lesters, as Benjamin had done in the days of Isaac Lester. Like Benjamin, Garland had a good head for business and realised the need to move with the times. It was probably partly his doing that the Lester fleet was modernised in the late 1790's and early 1800's. By 1806 it was reduced to 17 vessels but only one ship, the *Industry*, dated back to 1786 and she had been rebuilt in 1800. What the fleet now lacked in numbers it made up for in tonnage because four ships were in the range of 200-300 tons and the largest, the *Triton*, was of 323 tons. Garland recognised too that the great prosperity of the Newfoundland trade in the later years of the resumed war with France would probably not last and that it would be dangerous to extend his business any further. When the post-war depression came he did his best to maintain the trade, appearing with other Poole merchants before a Commons Select Committee on the trade in 1817 and trying hard to secure a reduction in the prohibitive fish duties imposed by the Spanish government. Ultimately however he realised that a reduction in the family's business commitments in Newfoundland was inescapable because even the 40,000 quintals of fish they were exporting were not sufficient to give an adequate return on the £80,000 they had invested in the trade.

As he wrote in 1821, "the establishments (in Newfoundland) are too numerous, too expensive and the contract system of giving such extensive credit to such numerous planters . . . can no longer be supported without risk of enormous loss or *at the very best* the necessity of investing again in the trade another capital of £15-20,000 at least, and this the situation of Europe in general as well as the prices of fish, oil, skins, etc. in common prudence forbids". Accordingly in 1820 he had disposed of some ships and the next year began to reduce the firm's shore establishments in Newfoundland by giving up all his fishing "rooms" and stores on the northern side of Trinity Bay. At the same time the planters had to accept restricted credit on the provisions and equipment supplied to them. In this way he was able to ensure that when the Garlands later came to give up their direct participation in the trade they were able to retire from it very much on their terms, while other less far-seeing merchants like the Spurriers and the Penneys were forcibly retired from the trade by bankruptcy.

Despite this reduction in the Garlands' commitments they still had extensive premises in Newfoundland centred on Trinity, and operated from fishing stations on the south shore of Trinity Bay as well as Bonavista, Bay de Verde and Greenspond. The Garland fleet in 1821 was still large too; it numbered 13 vessels: the *Amy* (183 tons), *Augustus* (186 tons), *Benjamin* (197 tons), *Dart* (84 tons), *Dolphin* (101 tons), *Garland* (269 tons), *George* (166 tons), *Hope* (93 tons), *Lester* (196 tons), *Maria* (184 tons), *Nelson* (242 tons), *Swift* (145 tons), and *Two Brothers* (224 tons). Two of these ships were later lost at sea: the *Nelson* was wrecked near Cherbourg on Christmas Day 1824 but the crew were saved and most of the cargo later salvaged, while the *Maria* was lost off Newfoundland in 1834, although her crew too survived. The brig *Lester* was a particularly fast ship and once in 1831 made the Atlantic crossing from Newfoundland in only 11 days. She was later to figure in a comparatively rare case of piracy. While sailing from Demerera (Guyana) to St John's, Newfoundland, in 1834 she was stopped, boarded and robbed by a pirate schooner with a crew of about 50 English, American, Spanish and Portuguese desperadoes, presumably from one of the islands in the Caribbean.

Just as Benjamin Lester had been able to relax so George Garland was aware too that life did not begin and end with business. He had become a well read man able to hold his own, as his letters show, with some of the intellectuals of the day. He showed great care too in the education of his children, some of whom were sent abroad to school. Nor was this concern for improvement limited to his own family; he was an earnest supporter of many of the societies and charities then created by the evangelical movement, such as the Poole Bible Society of which he was chairman. He also built and presented to the town in 1814 the Garland Almshouses at Hunger Hill where 12 of the community's deserving poor people could live. After his wife's death he also provided a fund to pay for the repair of the almshouses and to make a monthly allotment to their residents.

Garland inherited too the political power Benjamin Lester had wielded in the town. He served in most of the municipal posts, beginning as Overseer of the Poor in 1781 and ending as Mayor in 1788 and 1810. He also became one of the town's representatives in Parliament in 1801 when the death of General Stuart brought a by-election. At this time the well connected Stuart family of Highcliffe expected that the Government and the electors of Poole would willing accept General Stuart's son as his successor in the seat and were very much put out when George Garland announced his candidature and the Prime Minister, Addington, refused to intervene against him. In fact Addington showed a sensible realisation of the influence Garland possessed in the town and probably recognised too that many of the Poole electors did not altogether approve of the other member, John Jeffrey, another Poole merchant. Certainly the Lesters and Garland had never seen eye to eye with Jeffrey (whom Isaac Lester had once called "that insolent young puppy") and Garland probably saw a seat in Parliament partly as a means of curbing Jeffrey's power and ambition. As a politician Garland again demonstrated his willingness to move with the times and accepted the need for parliamentary reform as a means of reducing corruption in government and making Parliament more truly representative. After he retired from Parliament he played a leading role in securing some reforms in Poole Corporation which gave its members more freedom in the election of the Mayor and enabled it to be more business like and responsible in its administration of the town's affairs.

With such a large family to provide for, Garland like the Lesters before him began to buy more property. Those of his sons who lived in this country and were not working abroad had to be provided with suitable residences; George Garland himself had begun to play a part in county society and thus needed more property in keeping with his station. In any case country property was a sounder investment than the unstable Newfoundland trade in the eary 1800's. When John Jeffery sold his mansion, Sans Souci, out at Lytchett Minster in 1809, Garland considered buying it but eventually decided to purchase the Stone estate, overlooking Wimborne. Five years later he bought for £21,000 the much larger Leeson House estate at Langton Matravers, near Swanage. Both houses survive to this day, Stone Cottage as a private residence, and Leeson House as a Field Studies Centre maintained by Dorset County Council, and both houses still retain the improvements and embellishments which George Garland made in them, notably the cleverly re-used Flemish woodwork in Leeson House. (Certain of the features of Stone Cottage are also to be found in Upton House because George Garland advised his son-in-law Christopher Spurrier when he had this mansion built.)

While Garland never actually retired from business or public life to take his ease at Stone or Leeson House – the year before his death in 1825 in a road accident at Wimborne he served as High Sheriff of Dorset – in his later years he was able to rely on the work of his numerous sons in politics and the Newfoundland trade. Naturally they all became members of Poole Corporation as they came of age. Benjamin Lester Lester, the eldest, was Mayor in 1815 but had already entered the House of Commons as one of the Poole members in 1809, taking the seat that Christopher Spurrier so much desired. Lester Lester, with his father's help was able to fight off Spurrier's challenge and by the 1820's was so respected a figure that there was little danger that he would lose an election. In the tradition of his father he supported parliamentary and other reforms, although sometimes he went further than Garland would have liked. However, when parliamentary reform was achieved in 1832,

Lester Lester found that the bitter divisions in Poole politics were becoming unbearable and retired in 1835, hoping to indulge his taste for foreign travel. He died unmarried in Paris in 1838. Joseph Gulston Garland, one of twin second sons, followed a career in the Royal Navy, serving at first on the *Raisonnable* in the West Indies in 1795. Later in the war he was in Lisbon, Cadiz and North America. A Captain at the end of the Napoleonic wars he was later promoted to Rear Admiral. He also found time to play a part in Poole's affairs and in 1830 was the last member of the family to become Mayor. Like his brother he found that Poole in the 1830's became a petty, tedious and depressing place to live in and for many years until his death in 1854 lived out at Stone.

Francis Penton Garland, the other twin son, remained in Poole and for some time looked after the business which had belonged to Sir John Lester. All the other surviving sons went abroad to work in branches of the Newfoundland trade, one of them, Lester Garland, dying at Leghorn in 1798 at the age of 15 to the great grief of his father and mother. Another son, Augustus, later established a business in Leghorn. The two remaining sons, John Bingley Garland and George Garland (jun.) started work in Lisbon for the firm of Hart, Garland and Robinson which handled the Portuguese side of the Newfoundland trade but in 1819 were sent to Trinity to manage the fisheries. George Garland had become dissatisfied with the work of his agent there, David Durell, also from Poole, and suspected with justification that Durell was aiming at setting up business on his own account. His two sons were therefore sent to Newfoundland to ensure that the business there was properly managed in the difficult years of depression in the trade. Later he sent out the chief clerk in his Poole office, William Furnell, as an additional manager. Both of these sons remained in Newfoundland until the 1830's although John Bingley Garland came back to Poole on occasions and was elected Mayor in 1824. By his first marriage to a daughter of the Vallis family in Poole he acquired some of the Trinity property of the White family which had passed to the Vallises. His second wife came from the Read family, also established in Trinity as merchants in partnership with the Sleats of Poole.

When George Garland and later John Bingley Garland finally returned to Britain in the 1830's the direct connection between the family and Newfoundland was at last broken, although the Garlands retained their interest in the trade through the London firm of Robinson, Brooking and Garland, and a branch of the family which had settled in Portugal also remained in the trade until the end of the 19th century. By the 1860's the Newfoundland business had been moved from Trinity to Greenspond in an effort to avoid the effect of the restrictions imposed on English and foreign merchants by the Newfoundland government. The last Garlands to live in Newfoundland, however, left some permanent memorials to their stay there, not only in their generosity to churches there but in the part they played in the government of Newfoundland. They were concerned to modernise the government of the colony, and worked with

John Bingley Garland, 1791–1875, Mayor of Poole 1824.

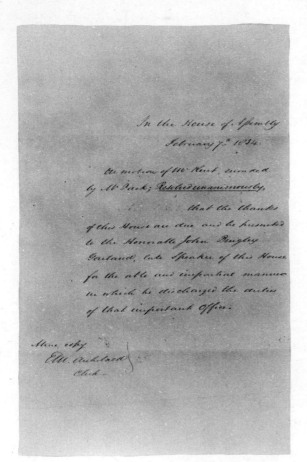

Copy of the resolution of the Newfoundland House of
Assembly thanking John Bingley Garland for
his services as Speaker of the House.

The Garland coat of arms
on the gatepost of Poole Cemetery.

Plaque commemorating J B Garland's gift of land.
The cemetery was consecrated on 17 February 1855 and
the first person to be buried there was
a Mr Bush, aged 88 years, interred on 2 March 1855.

The Garland Memorial Chapel in Poole Cemetery.

The Garland Almshouses at Hunger Hill.

The first Poole Library, presented to the town by Benjamin Lester Lester MP and W. F. S. Ponsonby MP in 1830. The site is now occupied by the offices of the Poole Harbour Commissioners.

A 19th century view of Trinity, Newfoundland. It was one of the earliest settlements made by the British in the island and is said to have been one of the few places there that resembled an English village.

their brother Benjamin Lester Lester and business partner G R Robinson, also an MP, to persuade the British Government to grant representative government to the colony in 1832. Fittingly it was the Garlands' brig *Lester* which brought the petitions for representative government from Newfoundland. John Bingley Garland was elected to the first House of Assembly as member for Trinity Bay and was shortly afterwards chosen as the first Speaker of the House.

At this same time the family's links with Poole were weakening. The Mansion House and other properties in the town which the Lesters and the Garlands had accumulated were either let or sold in the 1830's, for they were no longer needed. George Garland (jun.) died at Stanley Green shortly after his return home and John Bingley Garland went to live the life of a country gentleman at Leeson House and Stone. He had already served as High Sheriff of Dorset in 1827 and continued to play his part in county affairs; when he died in 1875 he was one of the oldest magistrates in the county. However, he did not forget the association between his family and Poole; in 1851 he gave a piece of land so that a company could be established to provide for a long felt need in the town – an additional cemetery, but because it proved impossible to set up a satisfactory company for this purpose, in 1854 he presented the 13 acres to the Burial Board of St James Church. The cemetery was opened in the same year and still includes the Garland memorial chapel built by J B Garland in 1857. He himself was buried there in 1875.

John Bingley Garland's first two sons, the next generation of the Garland family, continued to live in Dorset and the family took care to keep alive the name of Lester. Thus, in 1854, J B Garland's son Lester Garland took the surname Lester and later, to avoid the dying out of the name of Garland, his son in turn took the surname of Lester-Garland. Careers in the Church, the Army, the Civil Service and Medicine took the next two generations of George Garland's descendants away from Dorset to travel widely and live in Australia, New Zealand and India but in recent years the late Rev G H Lester-Garland and his sister, Miss E M Lester-Garland, have done much to foster the old associations between their family and both Poole and Newfoundland and have generously ensured that many mementoes of the Lesters and Garlands are available for us to see and study in Poole and Dorset.

Some of the buildings associated with these two families who played such a large part in shaping Poole's past have of course subsequently disappeared. The Garland Almshouses and the town's first library opposite Scaplen's Court, which Benjamin Lester Lester and his fellow MP presented to the community in 1830, are now but memories. After many vicissitudes however, the Mansion House has now regained much of its former glories. Out in Dorset, Stone Cottage still gazes down on Wimborne and Leeson House retains something of the atmosphere of a country gentleman's house, despite its many youthful residents. In the heart of old Poole itself, Benjamin Lester and his grandson are to be seen once again in the Guildhall, their portraits looking down on 20th century visitors to a building where they often came – to govern the town, to dispense justice, to fight elections and to join in the feast and toasts of the 18th and early 19th centuries.

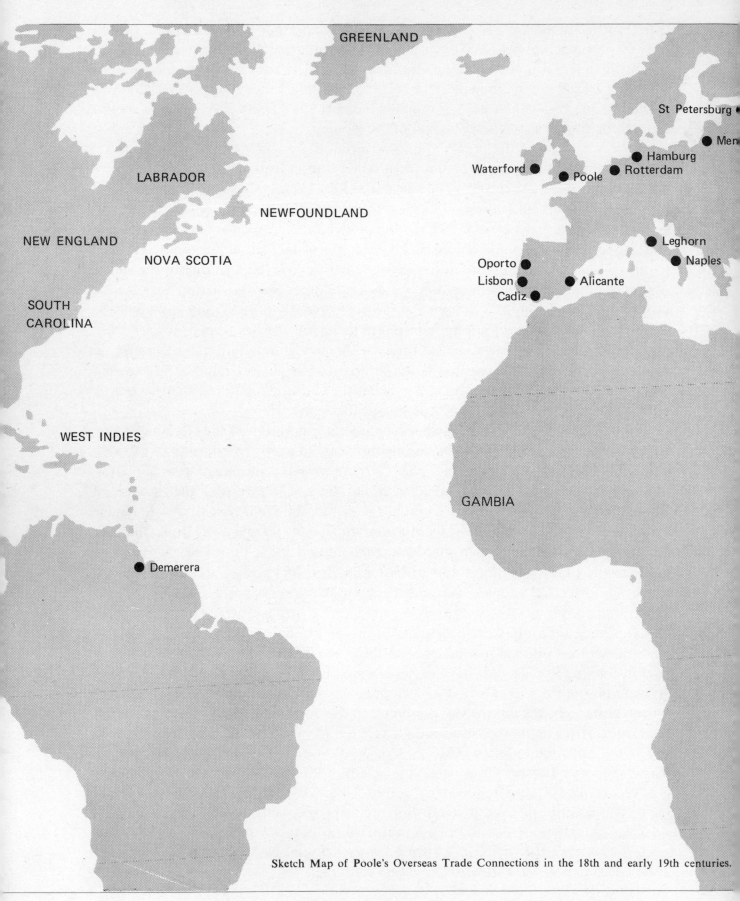

GREENLAND

St Petersburg

Men

LABRADOR

Hamburg

Waterford

Poole

Rotterdam

NEWFOUNDLAND

NEW ENGLAND

NOVA SCOTIA

Leghorn

Oporto

Naples

SOUTH
CAROLINA

Lisbon

Alicante

Cadiz

WEST INDIES

GAMBIA

Demerera

Sketch Map of Poole's Overseas Trade Connections in the 18th and early 19th centuries.

The Old Red Cow

The life of the Poole merchant John Masters in some ways forms a contrast with the careers of most of the other merchants of the town. It is true that like many of them he became very wealthy in the Newfoundland trade, but he was different in that he was actually born in Newfoundland and had much greater disadvantages to overcome in his early life before he could emerge as a successful merchant. As far as is known, he was also the only Poole merchant to live in a mansion which had previously served as an ale house – the Old Red Cow.

He was born either in 1687 or 1688 in Silly Cove, a fishing station on Trinity Bay. (The name no longer appears on maps of Newfoundland because in 1912 the inhabitants had the place renamed Winterton, resenting the implication of the previous name.) Masters's father, after whom he was named, was one of the "planters", those men who stayed in Newfoundland to carry on the fisheries in contrast to those who came out each year from the west of England and returned home at the end of each fishing season. The more or less permanent population of Newfoundland was then very small – in 1691 it was calculated that there were only 1,789 men, women and children living there, including 261 planters. Like other planters and merchants, John Masters Senior suffered a great deal from the French attacks on the island during the wars beginning in 1689, and was taken prison in a French raid. "Forty or fifty armed Frenchmen came over by land from Placentia to Silly Cove, surprised the inhabitants, killing three or four and took Mr John Masters out of his bed, rifled his house and carried him and his goods aboard a Jersey ship laden with fish, and sailed northwards." The unfortunate Masters escaped from the French, came to Poole in 1697 with his wife, son and four daughters, "and bought a low old house at the upper end of the High Street". Leaving his family there he returned to Silly Cove to recoup his fortunes only to be murdered shortly afterwards in a brush with the Indians.

His widow "to support the expense of Life set up an Ale house, the sign of the red cow in a low mean way," and the young John Masters was sent to school in Wimborne. When he was 13 his mother apprenticed him to William Taverner, then a captain of a Newfoundland ship. Masters rose to be a ship's mate and after a period as a planter became in 1715 the master of a small Bristol ship, the *Frome*, plying the Newfoundland trade from St John's. Sir Peter Thompson, who met him there, noted that "he was very industrious, split all his shore fish and I thought worked rather too much". Masters's hard work however soon made him prosper and in the 1720's he also started salmon fishing in the Salmonier River further south in the Avalon Peninsula. By the 1730's he was exporting large amounts of fish from St John's, partly for himself and partly for other merchants. About 1740 he had become wealthy enough to return to England permanently, leaving the Newfoundland end of the business in the hands of his Irish partner, Michael Ballard. He now married Sarah Taverner, the daughter of his former master and settled at Greenwich.

He was too enterprising an individual to be content with living the life of a successful merchant and determined to secure a seat in the House of Commons. Unfortunately, however, he was not on good terms with the Government and could not therefore get the support of the administration, then a vital need for an individual attempting to make an entry into Parliament. Masters had in fact quarrelled a great deal with William Keen, one of the New Englanders who had been appointed a magistrate in Newfoundland, where the British Government was gradually increasing the amount and authority of formal government at the expense of the power of the West Country merchants. Poole merchants had reacted particularly against this development and the Corporation had sent up a strong protest to London in 1731. By 1734 William Keen had become the *bête noire* of the wealthy and demanding Quaker merchant, Samuel White of Poole, who accused Keen of using his power improperly in the enforcement of the Navigation Acts which then regulated Britain's overseas trade. Keen, he later alleged, had picked on one of White's ships, because it was in competition with one of his own ships, and imprisoned the captain of it because he had found a small item of alleged contraband on board – a box of candles. Meanwhile, other ships escaped searches completely. John Masters had evidently intervened to try unsuccessfully to secure the release of the captain, and followed up this episode by undertaking the management of a fresh petition against what the merchants indignantly saw as oppression at the hands of the representatives of government in Newfoundland.

Lacking the right standing with Sir Robert Walpole's administration, Masters had to let the election of 1741 pass by and hope for better things in the next election in 1747. In the meantime he began to make preparations to return to Poole, with the aim of acquiring a parliamentary seat there. He had the old alehouse in the High Street rebuilt into a mansion at the cost of £1,500, but unfortunately it has not yet proved possible to identify this building. Having bought a second-hand chariot, he took up residence in his mother's old house late in 1746, and was soon appearing too in one of the more expensive pews in St James Church, in fact a pew previously occupied by the Rector's own family. (Like many Poole men, he also appears to have kept a connection with the dissenting chapel, and had a pew there too.)

At the same time he was naturally busy maintaining his trade with Newfoundland and in 1745 lost one of his ships, laden with brandy and building lime for Newfoundland, when it was driven ashore off Lyme Regis. He also spent much time acting as the spokesman for Poole and other West Country merchants in their dealings with the Government on matters of concern to the Newfoundland trade, apparently hoping to impress both the ministers and the merchants with his importance and competence so that he could gain the all-important Government backing in the next general election.

Placentia, an important centre for the French fisheries in Newfoundland which was ceded to the British in 1713.

St John's Newfoundland showing the fort. An 18th century print.

The country was by now engaged in a fresh war which had started as the "War of Jenkin's Ear" against Spain and had later become merged in the War of Austrian Succession involving France as well. The Newfoundland merchants were fearful that the French would repeat the successes they had in the earlier wars against Newfoundland ports and fishing stations and Masters, remembering his unfortunate father's alarming experience, did not need to be reminded of this danger. The merchants were also desperately anxious about the losses they were suffering to privateers – by the end of 1743 it was calculated that Poole had lost 31 ships of the total value of £39,800 as a result of the attacks of Spanish privateers. Early in 1740 Masters helped to secure the Government's agreement to fortify St John's and later helped persuade the Committee on Trade and Plantations to order defence works for Trinity Harbour as well, although on a rather parsimonious scale because the Committee specified that the work was to be done "at as little charge as the nature of the place will admit". Masters was also active in supporting the merchants' pleas for better naval protection of the Newfoundland fleets, like the petition sent up by Poole Corporation and merchants in 1744 which complained that only one 40-gun ship had been provided to convoy the 60 to 70 ships of the Newfoundland traders.

All this activity impressed many of the Poole merchants and in 1744 Masters was elected to the Corporation at the same time as Peter Thompson. However, some of the burgesses were wary of Masters and evidently feared that he would be a difficult man to control, as the town clerk's letter to Thompson shows. Later events in Poole were to demonstrate that these fears were only too correct! Not surprisingly too, the energetic way in which Masters badgered ministers and officials hardly endeared him to the Government. Moreover, Masters had apparently made himself a nuisance in another way. Good business man that he was, he had sought to make a profit from the fortification of St John's he had helped to bring about: he had obtained a contract from the Governor of Newfoundland to supply the provisions needed by the English labourers and the marines in the garrison of St Johns. Unfortunately for him, the British Treasury wanted to satisfy other claimants for Government favours by awarding the contract to them and they terminated Masters's contract in 1744. Clearly Masters was still a long way from obtaining the support of Government and his conduct since he returned to this country had only made it less likely that the administration would smile upon him.

Undeterred by this he made an effort at winning one of the Poole seats in 1747, doubtless spurred on by well-founded suspicions that Sir Peter Thompson was not only aiming at installing his friend, James West, Secretary to the Treasury and Recorder of Poole, in one Poole seat but would like to take the other one for himself. Masters and Sir Peter engaged in some ultra polite verbal fencing with one another, each solemnly declaring that they had no intention of standing while at the same time making their private arrangements to do this. Sir Peter was eventually returned for St Albans with his friend West while Masters came forward at Poole. According to Sir Peter, whose evidence may not be completely reliable, Masters spent more than £700 in trying to influence the members of the Corporation to

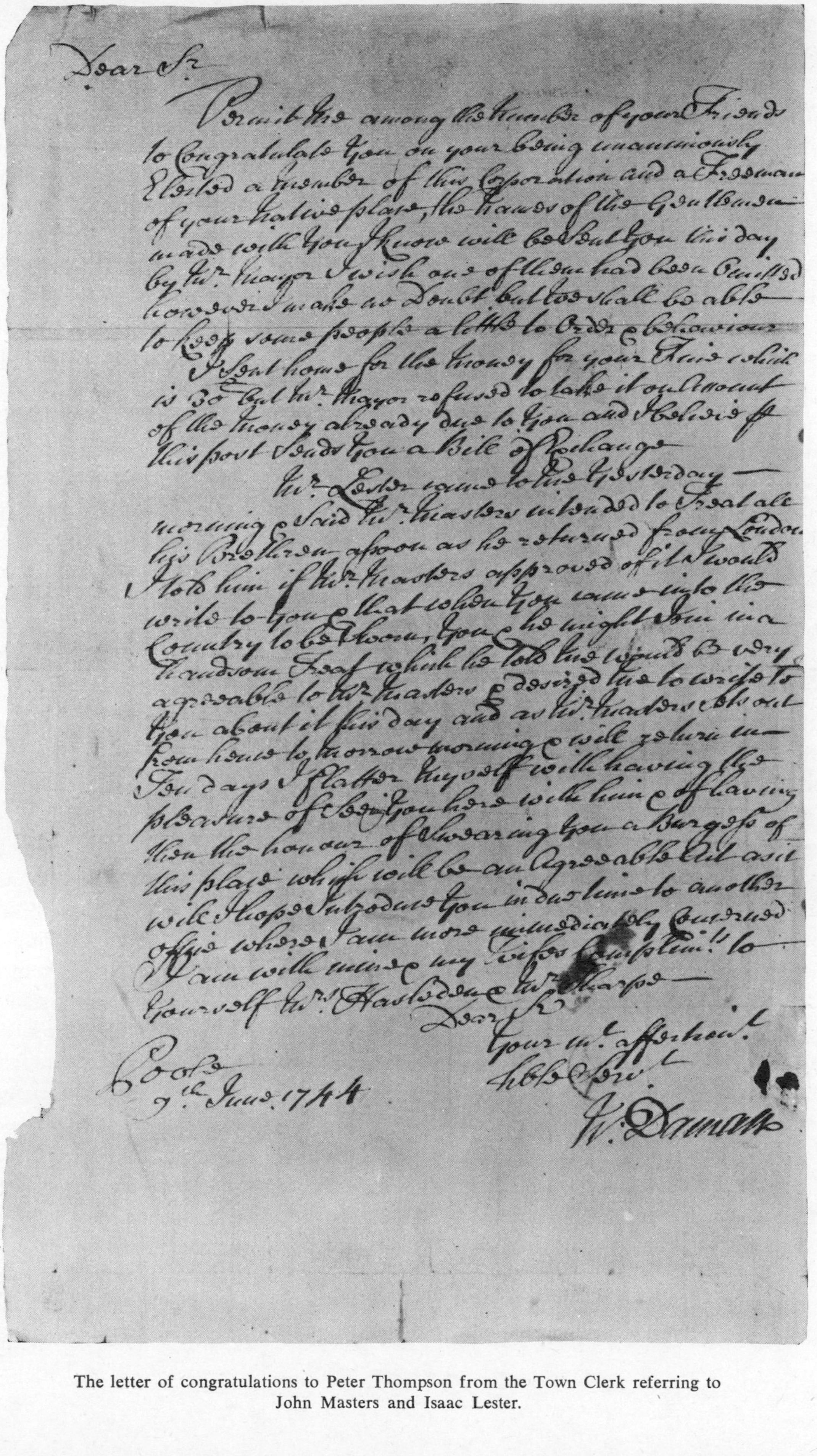
Dear Sir

Permit me among the number of your Friends to Congratulate you on your being unanimously Elected a member of this Corporation and a Freeman of your native place, the names of the Gentlemen made with you I know will be sent you this day by Mr. Mayor I wish one of them had been omitted however I make no Doubt but we shall be able to keep some people a little to Order & behaviour

I sent home for the money for your Fine which is 30 but Mr. Mayor refused to take it out of the money already due to you and I believe by this post sends you a Bill of Exchange

Mr. Lester came to me yesterday morning & said Mr. Masters intended to Treat all his Brethren as soon as he returned from London I told him if Mr. Masters approved of it I would write to you that when you came into the Country to be Freeman, you & he might Join in a handsom Treat which he told me would be very agreeable to Mr. Masters & desired me to write to you about it this day and as Mr. Masters is Sett out from home tomorrow morning & will return in Ten days I flatter myself with having the pleasure of seeing you here with him & of having then the honour of Swearing you a Burgess of this place which will be an Agreeable Act as it will I hope Introduce you in due time to another Office where I am more immediately Concerned

I am with mine & my Wifes Compliments to yourself Mrs. Hasleden & Mr. [illegible]

Dear Sir

Your most affectionate

Humble Servant

W. Damant

Poole

7th June 1744

The letter of congratulations to Peter Thompson from the Town Clerk referring to John Masters and Isaac Lester.

support him, but in the end had to give up the contest because the Government influence in favour of the successful candidates was too strong.

Nevertheless, Masters was successful in attracting the support of enough of the burgesses to make himself Mayor in 1748, but he broke with precedent because he had not previously served any of the junior offices in the Corporation to qualify himself to be Mayor, and his opponents in Poole unsuccessfully tried to dislodge him by starting a lawsuit. His influence continued to grow however, not just because of the force of his personality and his money but because he undoubtedly tried to do his best for the town. In particular he attempted to secure an Act of Parliament to legalise beyond any shadow of doubt the Corporation's right to charge dues for the use of the port and to make it possible for them to finance improvements in the quays and other facilities of the port. The Corporation at this time tried to collect these dues, claiming that they had an ancient right "from time beyond the Memory of Man" but the Wareham traders in particular, who understandably did not possess such good memories as the people of Poole, steadfastly resisted and avoided paying these dues. Since Wareham merchants were making increasing use of the quays and facilities at Poole, because the River Frome was silting up and becoming more difficult to navigate, and some Poole merchants were beginning to copy their resistance to paying the dues, Poole Corporation became more and more angry with their lack of power and welcomed Masters's initiative. Yet again, however, Masters failed, primarily because the inhabitants of Wareham managed to get the valuable support of Lord Shaftesbury in their campaign against the proposed addition to Poole Corporation's powers.

Despite this failure Masters continued to gather strength in Poole and by 1751 could count on the support of the Spurriers because when Alderman Timothy Spurrier became Mayor in that year it was claimed that he represented "the Independent Party of the Burgesses in the interest of the worthy John Masters Esq". This independence amongst the Poole electors was not to the liking of the portly and wealthy politician George Bubb Dodington, who had previously enjoyed such very great influence in the borough that it had once been called his "washpot". Dodington had a palatial country house, Eastbury, out at Tarrant Gunville, and in September 1752 he journeyed down to Poole in his coach to attend the election of the next Mayor, hoping to put a stop to the ambitions of the upstart Masters. However, not even Dodington's considerable presence was sufficient to prevent John Masters from being elected for a second term of office by a majority of 13 votes, and Dodington returned to Eastbury, never to visit Poole again.

As the time for the mayoral election of 1753 drew near, Masters considered how best to prolong his control over the Corporation. Because he may have felt that the burgesses would not accept him as Mayor for a third year, he decided to put up one of his supporters, Aaron Durell, a shipbuilder, and rule through him instead, but on this occasion his political machinations caused actual fighting to break out in the Guildhall at the installation of the new Mayor.

126

Masters had secured the election of Aaron Durell to succeed him by appealing to the majority of the ordinary burgesses while his opponents had elected George Hyde by following the customary method of nomination through the Aldermen. When the two would-be Mayors and their respective supporters met for the ceremony of swearing in, the two rival candidates tried to seat themselves simultaneously in the mayoral chair "on which a great disturbance ensued, and one Ballard, an Irishman, Mr Masters' partner in Newfoundland, not regarding the laws and customs of this nation, jumped upon the table and with great Fire and Indignation advanced towards Mr George Tito, the Sheriff, collar'd him and struck him in the face upon which Mr Hyde the Mayor read the proclamation against Rioters". According to Masters's account of the episode, however, it had been the Sheriff who had first jumped up on the table "and was followed by some of his troublesome adherents who made a great noise". Ballard, who Masters claimed "was no stranger to the Laws and Customs of this country", had merely followed suit in order to protect Masters from Tito, while Masters himself had soon ended the "slight skirmish" and "made use of persuasive language for peace, on which the fray soon subsided".

Masters evidently won this battle at the Guildhall because a majority of the ordinary burgesses were on his side and he had the town clerk, William Humfrey, in his pocket. His opponents were at first determined to dislodge Durell and end Masters's reign by insisting that the election had not been conducted according to precedent. They demanded that "Mr Masters will also please to set forth (without having recourse to his usual polite phrases of dirty pitiful Dogs) why he should attempt to break the ancient and immemorial usages and rights of this Corporation", and vowed that they would put a stop to "the arbitrary claims of insolent power and NEWFOUNDLAND MONARCHY". Despite this bold language they did not press home the lawsuit they started against Masters, and his man Durell was allowed to continue as Mayor.

This was virtually Masters's last throw in politics. He had hoped to attach himself to the opposition group which had formed in national politics around Frederick the Prince of Wales, and so at last obtain one of the Poole seats at the next election. (An acquaintance of his, Admiral Thomas Smith, a former Governor of Newfoundland, was to be groomed for the other seat.) Unfortunately for Masters and the other political malcontents of the day "poor Fred" unexpectedly died and his party and their hopes were ruined. When the election came in 1754 Masters thus had to content himself with tamely supporting the Government candidates but characteristically tried to be the leader of the party. The next year he died while on a visit to London but was brought back to Poole for burial.

Many of his contemporaries probably disagreed with some of the qualities his widow saw in him and had inscribed on his memorial in St James – in particular the references to his "general benevolence to all mankind" and the "universal esteem" in which he was held. As far as we are able to judge him, we may agree with Sir Peter Thompson's view of him as "a fine figure of a man – only wanted polishing". Masters achieved a great deal in overcoming his early disadvantages by dint of sheer

To the Memory of
Mr JOHN MASTERS Merch.t
of this Town, Whose tender
Affection to his Wife, Sincerity
to his Friends, Liberality to the Poor, &
great Benevolence to All mankind,
render'd him Universally esteemed.
This Monument was erected by his
sorrowful Relict as a token of her
Everlasting Love for him.
He died in London June 20.th
A.D. 1755
In the 64.th Year of his Age,
& lies buried near this place.

"Your most honourable Servant John Masters"

industry and determination but, understandably in view of his past, he did not realise that to be successful in politics he needed to temper his hard work and resolution with tact and patience – that the bluff manners of a Newfoundland planter and merchant would not easily mix in the contemporary world of political compromise. For all that, he played a valuable part in Poole politics and blazed a trail for others to follow – in 1756 the Corporation obtained their Act of Parliament for the harbour and ten years after his death, Joshua Mauger, a free-booting Poole merchant something like John Masters, at last broke the hold of outsiders on the Poole seats in the Commons. As for the burgesses of Poole, immediately after Masters's death they swore that they would never be so divided again – and it was at least two years before they were at one another's throats once more!

Rolles

Beech Hurst

Built in 1798, Beech Hurst in the High Street was one of the last of the great mansion houses to be built in Poole. Its owner, Samuel Rolles, was known as "a gentleman" by this time, but in his younger days, like his father before him, he had been a ship's master for his powerful relatives, the White family. Samuel strengthened this connection by marrying his cousin Amy White when she was widowed, and was able to build Beech Hurst with his share of the enormous fortune of the White family.

The Whites could trace their family line in Poole back to the early 1600's at least and may have been descended from the family of White which played a large part in the town's history in the first half of the previous century, serving as Mayors and Members of Parliament and leading the defence of the Roman Catholic religion against the Protestant reformers. If they were so connected their religious faith had undergone a radical change for the later Whites were devout members of the Quaker Meeting House in Poole, an influential group of about 100 people in the 1700's.

The Whites were sea captains and in 1609 one of the family appears in the records of Poole's Admiralty Court which had long existed to defend the rights of the townspeople to control their valuable harbour. Before the end of this century the Whites had graduated from being merely the masters of ships and had begun to build up very extensive business interests as merchants. Samuel White (1642-1720) of Lagland Street married into the Newfoundland trade by choosing as his wife Mary Taverner, a member of another Poole family which was already well established in Newfoundland as planters in the fisheries. A Mrs Taverner who is listed in a census of the fishery made in 1675 was one of the few women ever to take on the arduous occupation of planter and the family, some of whom were Quakers, were to supply brides for other Poole merchants – the Lesters and John Masters. The next generation of Whites also made marriages which helped to advance their interests in trade: Samuel White (1674-1747) married a member of the Tucker family of Weymouth, leading merchants there who obtained one of the Weymouth seats in the Commons and were able to use their influence to help the Whites on occasions in their dealings with the Government; William White (1671-1749) who lived in the High Street, was married twice, to a Skinner and a Bennett, both Poole families with interests in the Newfoundland trade; Joseph White (1685-1771) also of the High Street, chose Elizabeth Nickleson from another Poole merchant family with strong connections with Pennsylvania.

By enterprise, industry and thrift and judicious marriages, the family was able to acquire a very large stake in the Newfoundland trade, based on the fisheries of Bonavista and Trinity Bays and Fogo Island. Joseph White had premises in Trinity where he was partnered by his relative Vallis and employed another Poole man, Captain Samson Mifflin, as his agent. By 1731 port records in Poole show that Samuel White imported "65 tuns of Oyle on board severall vessells and 300 qtrs of Oats on Commission". However, trade with Newfoundland was only one aspect of the family's business in the early 1700's; their ships were not only to be found off-loading cod fish in the ports of Spain and Portugal but at Barbados in the West Indies, Virginia, and nearer home in Baltic, Dutch and French ports, fetching and carrying whatever cargo was profitable. It appears that the Whites were able to develop this extensive trade partly as a result of the Government contracts they enjoyed for carrying supplies during the wars against France between 1689 and 1713. In Poole itself Samuel White also established a malting business, which was situated in Church Street.

These varied enterprises were exceedingly profitable and the fortunes amassed by the family in the 18th century were the largest by then accumulated by Poole merchants. When Joseph died in 1771, "he was possessed of a real fortune of £150,000 which he left, a few legacies excepted, to his nephew Samuel". When this fortunate nephew in turn died in 1797 it was reported that he was worth nearly £200,000. The Whites' business in Poole was rated for £50,000 in the Poor Rate of 1773, a figure nearly double that calculated for the prosperous business of the Lester brothers in the same year. Quite apart from their business premises, the family had become sizable property owners in the town and owned tenements in Lagland Street, Church Street, Market Street and White Bear Lane.

While Joseph White was content to remain living in the High Street, sometime early in the 1700's his brother Samuel moved from comparatively humble quarters in Lagland Street to a newly-built mansion house more befitting the family's growing wealth and status in the town. This house, on the north side of New Street, was demolished about ten years ago but in 1973-74 Poole Museum's archaeological unit excavated the site, with the aid of numerous volunteers. Many fascinating relics of the family's life in the house were retrieved, especially from rubbish pits. Bottles and bottle seals bearing the initials of their relatives, the Vallis family, and the Carters, a family of wealthy Hamworthy rope-makers, who were close to the Whites, were unearthed. The prize item however was a particularly fine Chinese porcelain tea set which has been skilfully reconstructed by Poole Museum. In all, there is much evidence that the family's public reputation of parsimony did not prevent them from indulging in some luxurious living at home.

These great fortunes and precious possessions were not acquired without a great deal of enterprise and hard work; the family appear to have been always watchful for any opportunity to advance their business. An illustration of this appears in the papers of a leading merchant in Charleston, South Carolina, who had dealings with Samuel White in 1757. White's ship, *Samuel and Dove*, commanded by Captain

Botley, came into Charleston early that year from Newfoundland, possibly with "refuse", or inferior fish for sale to plantation owners for feeding their slaves. White did not apparently normally trade in Charleston but would have known from the Jolliffes, who were heavily committed to this trade, that there were good profits to be made in carrying rice, especially from South Carolina to Portugal or Spain. However, he was not only anxious to secure a cargo of rice but keen too to find out if "white oak staves" were available. In the event he was disappointed but the Charleston merchant was able to put together a cargo for his ship by stressing that "we have been informed by indifferent Persons who know her that very few vessels in England will sail faster than She", and in April the *Samuel and Dove* sailed for Lisbon "under convoy of the *Kennington* and *Nightingale*, men of war", with 180 barrels and 35 half barrels of rice in her cargo.

Like other Poole merchants the Whites also had to take great risks in order to amass their fortune. Samuel White's sloop *Jenny* went down with all her crew in a bad storm in Newfoundland in 1768. They lost very heavily during the Seven Years War (1756-63) when it is said that Joseph White lost all but one of his 14 ships and had not insured any of them. One of these vessels was the sloop *Thomas*, which disappeared with her crew of 23 men on a voyage to Goose Bay in Labrador. At this time too, Sir Peter Thompson noted that the Whites had lost no less than 12,000 quintals of fish in Lisbon, forfeited when Portugal was forced into the war on the side of the French and Spaniards in January 1762. An earlier war in the century had caused them great anxieties: in 1743 Samuel White was alarmed at the prospects of France becoming involved in the war with Spain because losses to Spanish privateers had been so great, while the next year he complained, "We have several ships now ready for sailing for the land (Newfoundland) but cannot here of any convoy. They tell us theirs one but don't say his name, where she is nor when she sail which if we has not one soon the French war to will rewen our voiges – as indeed their was a great deal of money lost last year by the Convoy staying so long". Personal worries intruded too, for his own son, then aged 15, had been carried off by a French privateer into Brest or Dinan and he had to make arrangements for him to be supplied with money and exchanged for a French prisoner of war if possible. During the Seven Years War the Whites were involved in a further prisoner of war problem which illustrates how far these exchanges were from the methods of "total war" waged in the 20th century and how near they were to the earlier customs of chivalry. William Waldren, a Poole merchant, had been captured by the French and then exchanged for a French prisoner but the French, having received their countryman, then demanded that a French privateer captain should be returned instead. If this could not be arranged Waldren would have to return to France but it was possible that the French would accept a merchant captain instead! Unfortunately, however, we do not know exactly how this episode ended, whether Waldren had to return to France and an irate but too humble Frenchman had to return unwillingly to this country!

Fishing rooms on Conception Bay, Newfoundland, one of the areas in the north of the Avalon peninsula exploited by Poole Merchants.
The sketch was drawn in 1857 by the Rev William Grey (1819–72) a missionary in Newfoundland who later lived for a short time in Bournemouth.
Information supplied by Dr F Jones of the Dorset Institute of Higher Education.

The brig Union of Poole entering Leghorn Harbour.

New Street in the 1960's, shortly before the demolition of the buildings on the north side of the street which included Samuel White's house.

New Street in 1976. The site of the White's house and its neighbours is now occupied by Cinnamon Court.

Thrift was another prime reason for the White's success as merchants, although their contemporaries used stronger terms such as "Quaker misers"! It is only too clear that they had an unfortunate reputation as grasping individuals amongst their fellow townsmen. A contemporary observer noted their "absolute parsimony" and told how Samuel White was accustomed to cut an irregular piece of bacon from the flitch hanging in his kitchen when he left the house in the care of his solitary maid servant. He would lock this piece of bacon away carefully and on his return fit it on to the flitch to assure himself that the servant had not stolen any bacon from it during his absence! Isaac Lester, the Poole merchant, once remarked, "that family can ask anything but will do nothing for anybody". This might be discounted as mere jealousy on his part but evidence from a Newfoundland missionary confirms his view. This clergyman complained bitterly in 1774 that his house in Trinity was over-shadowed by part of the Whites' factory there, "built by order of a Quaker miser from Poole". It may be noted too that the Charleston merchant who handled the cargo of the *Samuel and Dove* in 1757 was evidently surprised that her captain had no money, or means of getting money, to pay for the expenses of the ship while in port. He sent a bill for £95 7s. 8d. to Samuel White but was able to sweeten the pill by telling him that some of the expenses should be deducted from the crew's wages because they had carelessly sunk a ballast lighter in Charleston Harbour.

Since the family were Quakers they did not serve in any of the senior posts in Poole Corporation and this meant that they could save money which they would otherwise have had to spend on elections, feasting and other municipal duties of the day. However, they were far too wealthy and important a group to be excluded from the Corporation by the application of the strict letter of the law and as members of the Corporation in many ways thus gained the advantages while avoiding the full responsibilities of power. Not unexpectedly they played a part in the administration of the Poor Law in the town – Samuel White was one of the trustees of the newly built Workhouse in 1739 – but their principal activity was at election times, when their block of family votes, normally five in number, and the votes of their relatives and friends such as the Rolles and Vallis families, counted for a great deal. Thus, whatever their fellow merchants and burgesses thought of them privately, they eagerly canvassed the Whites' votes and in 1784, for example, Joseph Gulston (jun.) lost his seat for Poole partly because he and his "manager", Benjamin Lester, could not persuade the Whites to vote for him.

Great wealth and power could not however provide sons to carry on the White family's career; when Samuel White died in 1797 only two male Whites appear to have been left and since neither of them had sons, the White family proper came to an end in the early 19th century. The Whites had already experienced some private disasters; for example, Joseph White's daughter Elizabeth is recorded as dying of a broken heart at the age of 22 back in 1737, but unfortunately no further details are available of this romantic and intriguing story. Nevertheless, the numerous marriages made by the Whites with other Poole families ensured that their inheritance of both

The Quaker Meeting House in Prosperous Street in the 19th century. The building survives in a much altered form as the Lagland Street Boys' Club.

Chinese porcelain tea-set found on the site of Samuel White's house in New Street.

Plaque at the rear of Beech Hurst
showing the date of its building and the initials of Samuel Rolles.

Beech Hurst on the 1888 Ordnance Survey Town Plan. Despite the erection of the
Public Library the mansion still retained much of its splendid grounds.

138

blood and wealth was carried forward at first by such families as the Jeffreys, Vallises, Rolles and Seagers and later by the Garlands, Drivers, Steeles and Biddles.

John Jeffrey (MP for Poole 1796-1810) was the son of the Quaker Walter Jeffrey of Exeter who had married into the White family in 1751. Already a merchant of some consequence in the town, he together with Peter Street, the merchant related to the extensive Jolliffe family, inherited Joseph White's Newfoundland business. They do not appear to have made the success of the business which Joseph White had achieved and by the early 19th century this once great share in the trade was in decline.

Samuel White left his Newfoundland property to Samuel and John Rolles, Samuel Vallis and his nephew. The Vallis connection was founded by the marriage of Samuel Vallis to Love, one of the elder Samuel White's daughters – her sister Dove either did not choose, or perhaps was not asked, to marry and remained a spinster. Samuel Vallis was a Quaker sea captain who worked for the Whites in Newfoundland as well as commanding their ships, and in 1751 was master of the sloop *Charles and Elizabeth*. The last male Vallis died in 1808 and Samuel's grand-daughter Deborah later married John Bingley Garland, the eminent son of George Garland, the leading Newfoundland merchant and a famous figure in Poole politics and society. In this way part of the Whites' Newfoundland business came to be merged with that of the Garlands.

Two years before Love's marriage, her sister Sarah had married John Rolles, another Quaker sea captain, who was working for the Whites by 1744 when he was caught in Dunkirk by the outbreak of war with France. In 1751 he commanded their brigantine the *Samuel and John*. It was his eldest son Samuel who built Beech Hurst with his share of the White's inheritance but he did not live long to enjoy his impos- ing residence for he died in 1809. The house subsequently passed to his daughter (another Dove) who lived there with her husband, Isaac Steele. The Steeles played a part in Poole politics on the Conservative side and are remembered as benefactors of St James Church. In September 1833, a local newspaper reported how they were greeted on their return from a continental holiday by "a merry peal of bells".

Thereafter the house appears to have passed to a surgeon, Dr Alfred Crabb, and by 1880 had been bought by Philip Budge, a Cornishman who made a successful career in Poole as a solicitor. He served as mayor on three occasions late in Victoria's reign and as H P Smith noted "no native could have proved a stouter champion of the traditions of our ancient borough". He was the last individual to live in Beech Hurst which, like other High Street houses became less desirable as a residence and more convenient for use as an office. When the Public Library was built between 1887 and 1890 its site was carved off the picturesque grounds of Beech Hurst which once extended well down Mount Street. In the present century the mansion lost its shading trees and suffered the indignity of finding itself backed by the Gasworks. Fortunately it has nevertheless survived its odorous neighbour and, known within living memory by Poole people as "White's place", still stands as a monument to the Whites and the Rolles.

House Flag

Seal 92 tons

Commerce 127 tons

Enterprise 155 tons

Dispatch 103 tons

John Colborne & Co.

There were two families of Colborne in Poole in the 18th and 19th centuries and, in each, the favourite boy's name seems to have been John. There were, therefore, quite a number of John Colbornes in Poole in this period. One of the branches of this family made their home in Poole but the other family, though operating a sizeable merchant's business from the port of Poole, kept its roots in Sturminster.

The Poole part of the family of Colbornes seems to have made it first impact in Poole with Samuel Colborne who had premises in Strand Street, premises which at that time stretched through to the quay. Samuel Colborne himself therefore might well have had something to do with the maritime business of Poole. He seems to have been fairly well-to-do and to have had some standing elsewhere for it was almost certainly this Samuel Colborne who, in 1765, had already been the worshipful master of a masonic lodge and as such acted as a consecrating officer at the inauguration of the first masonic lodge in Poole, the Amity, at the Lion and Lamb Inn in Salisbury Street in 1765. It was, too, almost certainly his son, John Colborne, who joined the lodge in the first year of its existence.

The suspicion that Samuel Colborne was a successful man is reinforced by the fact that John Colborne was well-educated and as H P Smith in his "History of the Lodge of Amity" shows, he was soon taking a leading part in the newly-formed lodge. In 1767 he was made the treasurer of the lodge and, the following year, his scholarship was recognised by the Poole Corporation who chose him to be the schoolmaster of the old Free School of Poole, which was then in Thames Street near the Mansion House there.

On John Colborne's appointment to this post on 19th May 1768 the Corporation promised "to use our best endeavours that the usual salary of £20 per annum be allowed to him as customary". If it was not for the subsequent history of this John Colborne we might have been tempted to think that anyone taking such a position with such a faint undertaking as to the payment of his salary must have been a man of means. Actually, if John Colborne did not know it already, it is likely that his fellow brethren in his lodge, such as Joshua Mauger and Samuel Spratt, who were burgesses, would have been able to tell him that the Corporation never intended to pay the salary at all. The Corporation had, by this time, established it as a custom that the two members of parliament for Poole paid the salary of the town's schoolmaster, for the Corporation had found other uses for the Harbin and Robert's legacies which they had received for educational purposes.

Thus it was always problematical when John Colborne would receive his princely stipend. At one time Benjamin Lester was called in to help find and remind Joseph Gulston (jun) MP of his liability, when the MP had fallen on hard times and it was feared that John Colborne could continue no longer the education of the 22 boys then under his care.

John Colborne's education and his fine calligraphy did, though, enable him to earn small extra amounts of money. The Lodge of Amity helped out in getting him to transcribe their by-laws.

The 18th century was a time of very heavy drinking as well as of swearing and gambling, and some of the by-laws of the Lodge were directed towards abating these practices, at least during Lodge meetings. The by-laws specified various fines to be levied on the brethren for transgressing. It is possibly not too surprising that the Lodge funds gained little from the fines for flouting the regulation as to moderation in drinking. If any brother overstepped the mark it is likely that his brethren were by that time at least in an indulgent frame of mind. However, the by-laws in regard to swearing and wagering were enforced regularly and the chief offender against the by-law in regard to wagering was none other than the treasurer of the Lodge who, after meticulously writing out the "Bye Laws and Regulations of the Lodge of Amity" must have known them better than anyone else! John Colborne conscientiously and regularly entered such receipts as "Nov. 1, 1769. To Self – Two to one who will lay – Fine 2d.".

1780 was the high-water mark of John Colborne's life: in that year he was not only made the Worshipful Master of the Lodge of Amity but he was also elected the Deputy Grand Master of the Provincial Lodge of Dorset.

Shortly afterwards everything seems to have gone wrong for John Colborne. Whether this was due to his salary not having been paid or his apparently incorrigible predeliction for gambling or ill-health we shall probably never known. However, it is not improbable that his fall from grace was occasioned by his gambling, for his brethren in the Lodge seem to have been quite unsympathetic to his plight. By this time they had passed a further regulation to the effect that if a member had missed six consecutive Lodge meetings he could not be re-admitted to the Lodge unless he had first paid a fine of up to £1 1s. 0d. John Colborne missed six consecutive meetings in 1786 and was unable to pay the fine which his brethren levied on him. In August that year the brethren of the Amity Lodge formally expelled their past worshipful master and previous treasurer. In the following October, John Colborne died at his home in High Street. There was, too, another John Colborne many years later, a linen draper who occupied 120 High Street, Poole, but the John Colborne, the merchant of Poole, was of the earlier Sturminster branch of the family.

William Colborne was a merchant who in the late 18th century owned and occupied a store for exports and imports in Strand Street and traded with Newfoundland. Even as late as 1811 he was rated for only two vessels in Poole, the *Charlotte* of 182 tons and the *Pellow* of 88 tons but, even so,

The south side of Twillingate, the 'Northern Capital' where John Colborne & Co had its Newfoundland headquarters. Notice the fishermen's 'Rooms' built out to sea.

Exploits in Notre Dame Bay. The 'flakes' for drying the cod fish are shown in the right foreground of the photograph.

143

the amount of stock for import and export which he held was then about half as much as that of a moderate sized merchant in Poole, such as Robert Slade.

William Colborne must have increased his business greatly in the last few years before he retired, for in 1821 the firm owned five vessels which were registered and rated in Poole. They were the *Thomas and Rebecca* (61 tons), the *Dorset* (146 tons), the *Liberty* (185 tons), the *Enterprise* (155 tons) and the *Dispatch* (103 tons).

However, in or about 1821, William Colborne retired to live at Sturminster and the firm then became known as John Colborne & Co. Andrew Pearce, who had come from Piddleton to work in Poole, then ran the firm with John Colborne but made frequent visits to "the old gentleman in Sturminster".

Even before the firm became that of "John Colborne" it was well established and successful. It had its own planters living in Newfoundland and doing most of the cod fishing for the firm even though the firm appears to have done most of the seal "fishing" for itself. Their planters drew on the credit of the cod they hoped to catch the following spring to see them through the long months of waiting for the next fishing season. Their credit for their future catches had also to be invoked to set themselves up with the fishing gear and salt necessary to cure the fish.

John Colborne dealt through Twillingate with fishing bases around the bay such as Burnt Island. He appointed a manager in Twillingate, Elias Pearce, the son of his Poole manager, Andrew Pearce and, it seems, his elder son Andrew Pearce managed the outstation at Exploits on Burnt Island. He also appointed agents to act for him in Europe and the West Indies to deal with the sale of the fish there. His main European agent was Luiz Antonio de Souza at Figueira da Faz, a port on the Portuguese coast about half-way between Oporto and Lisbon.

Though they could perhaps only suspect it at the time, for the Newfoundland trade had always fluctuated greatly, the trade was past its peak when John Colborne and Andrew Pearce took it over in 1821. There were recurrent problems which sent Andrew Pearce regularly off through Blandford to Sturminster to see William Colborne or to Bristol and other ports to try to resolve difficulties, as well as frequent visits to Twillingate.

These journeys in the early 19th century took a long time. In December 1822 for instance, when Andrew Pearce was returning from a visit to his agent-son in Twillingate, bad weather caused their vessel to have to lay-to in a storm for eight days. They had called in at Waterford where, according to Andrew Pearce, the whole crew had been affected by the fumes of the bogs there, and the mate had had to "lie by" on his return to Poole. Their journey had taken them, with their five day stay at Waterford, no less than 46 days.

The management of even a medium-sized merchanting business such as that of John Colborne was a complicated job even in prosperous days in the trade. Communication between Poole and Newfoundland was only as quick as a sailing vessel could go and communication between either end of their business and the sailing ships was slow and haphazard or sometimes virtually non-existant. On an urgent call from Elias Pearce, the manager at Twillingate, for more salt, for instance, the best

A drawing of St John's with sailing ships at anchor made by the Rev W Gray in 1857.

Petty Harbour, 10 miles south of St John's.

that could be done from Poole was for a letter to be sent by the next vessel sailing to Newfoundland to tell Elias Pearce that Mr Colborne was sending the *Thomas and Rebecca* with the fish that had been landed at Poole from the *Commerce* to Portugal and, as soon as the *Thomas and Rebecca* had discharged the fish there, it "will proceed to you with salt".

It was a similar story a few years later on an urgent call being finally received at Poole for supplies of meat to be sent to Twillingate. "As pork is rather scarce with you", was the reply going back with the next sailing ship, "Capt Buck will hasten out from Ireland as fast as possible".

A further great difficulty in the efficient running of their business in those days was that John Colborne or Andrew Pearce never knew what the demand for their produce was likely to be from week to week or what price it was likely to fetch. The best Andrew Pearce could tell his son in Twillingate when he wrote to him in 1823 was to say that the *Thomas and Rebecca* had gone to Figueira and was then going direct to him at Twillingate. When the brig arrived there the captain would be able to tell him what the price of fish was then in Figueira and he would be able to judge how best to deal with what fish he then had.

The merchants of St John's, too, by the time John Colborne owned the firm, were increasing their hold on the trade of Newfoundland at the expense of the Poole merchants in the outports of Newfoundland, for many of the English business houses had transferred their business to St John's from England during the Napoleonic wars. John Colborne and Andrew Pearce clearly resented this transfer but still found it necessary to deal with "the St John's gentlemen", as they sarcastically referred to them for, not being used to middlemen, they never thought they had received enough for their produce. If their own vessels could not be spared to take their seal oil they would charter a vessel to take it to Liverpool rather than sell it to the Water Street merchants of St John's.

There were, also, other difficulties for John Colborne, struggling in the 1820's to keep his business thriving. There was a dearth of seamen, partly through the earlier deprivations of the press gangs in the Napoleonic wars, and partly because of the great numbers of ships and men which had been captured by the French and Spaniards earlier. Andrew Pearce considered himself lucky when he recruited some seamen in 1823. He wrote to his son in Twillingate: "The *Dispatch* will take freight to Twillingate as soon as she has arrived from Lisbon and bring out passengers and then you'll be able to divide them with Mr Bartlett as there are some good hands, or expected to be so—and you can fit out for cruising and the fishing as usual . . .".

Even in that time of peace there were the usual troubles of rumours of wars and shut markets to add to the newer problems of the trade. In 1823 the possibility of war between France and Spain, however, for once actually helped them, for the French kept their fleet of fishing vessels in their ports in case of war breaking out, in the same way as the English had used embargo warrants earlier. This left the Newfoundland fishermen from the "western adventurers" without any French competition. Andrew Pearce wrote to his son to tell him: "There seems to be a likelihood of war between France and Spain", he wrote. "France wants to dictate a mode of government for Spain, and have a large army on the Frontiers, but Spain seems to be determined to oppose them, and it seems as if the French won't visit Newfoundland this season". There was always the chance of war, though, as Andrew Pearce pointed out. "If the French get too much on, I expect that John Bull must take part with Spain as that country and Portugal are on good terms with us."

But wars were not often good news to the merchants, even if they were only civil wars and disturbances. By 1832 trade had worsened considerably and John Colborne was having to take gambles like all his predecessors before him. In that year Portugal's misrule and constitutional quarrels between the Septembrists and Carlists had led to the port of Lisbon being closed to all shipping, but the *Seal* and the *Dove* were loaded with fish and sent to Lisbon. "At present no vessels are allowed to enter", wrote Andrew Pearce, "but I hope ere they appear Pedro will be in possession".

That year, too, John Colborne and Andrew Pearce were worried about the extent of the credit which the resident fishermen in Newfoundland were wanting to draw on the firm. Poor prices had left their credit with John Colborne strained as the planters had drawn on credit to supply themselves and their families through the long cold winter. Andrew Pearce felt he had to go out to Newfoundland himself to look after the firm's interests, but could not be sure that his ship would get him there before the fishing season had started, so he wrote a letter to his son to warn him. "It's most likely before my arrival you'll have to fit out the Planters", he wrote, "but you must be careful how you go. Salt they can't have too much of – if they can use it. But with other things you must do as well as you can with them so as not to let them dig too deep."

By September 1832 things were getting quite desperate for the firm of John Colborne. Andrew Pearce, back in Poole, could not understand why men both at Poole and in Newfoundland were apparently more concerned with Reform of Parliament and the establishment of representative government in Newfoundland than the disarray in which the trade of Newfoundland then was. The state of the fishery and the basis of their very livelihood seemed to him to have taken a very poor second place in their thoughts to their hopes of Reform. Even the disastrous fire which had consumed the town of Harbour Grace in Newfoundland at the time in no way seemed to reduce the rejoicing in Newfoundland at the passage in England of the Reform Bill in 1832.

Andrew Pearce wrote to his son. "A message from St. John's just in," he said, "reports Harbour Grace to be destroyed by fire. By a St John's paper I notice great rejoicing had taken place at Twillingate from the passing of the Reform Bill. It would have been far more pleasing had they reported well of the Fishery, – not a line to say if the *Seal* had left."

That was in September 1832 and the two men running the firm of John Colborne were coming to the end of their tether. The firm of John Colborne struggled on for

Sacred to the Memory of
ANDREW W. PEARCE
of Piddletown, Dorsetshire
Late Collector
of H. M. Customs of this Port
whose spirit resigned its mortal tenement
August the 17th, 1841
in the 70th year of his age.

The cod fish were prepared and laid out to dry in 'flakes' as shown here. This photograph was taken at Little Bay Island, Newfoundland.

another year or so but, finally, in June 1834 the end came. All the past successes of "the old gentleman" at Sturminster finally counted for nothing. The firm of John Colborne was declared bankrupt. Their struggles to keep their ships running profitably, even taking freight for anybody anywhere, of running fish to the West Indies and "to southward", had finally failed. When it came to the final sale of their last three vessels (the other six had already gone) the auctioneer offered the following vessels for sale: the schooner *Elizabeth*, 58 tons, built in Newfoundland; the brig *Enterprise*, 155 tons, British built; and the brig *Dove*, 142 tons, also built in Newfoundland.

It is very doubtful whether, in the market for sailing vessels in 1835, the auctioneer had a single serious bidder.

Andrew Pearce was 62 years old when the firm of John Colborne was made bankrupt. He had spent his life in sailing ships and in the trade. He did, though, know Twillingate from his visits to his eldest son Elias, who was the Colborne agent there. He was lucky, therefore, when he decided to emigrate to Newfoundland to join his three sons there, that he was able to obtain the position as collector of customs at Twillingate. His sons Elias and Frederick went to join Andrew, the second son, at Exploits only 15 miles away, to become planters to the merchants at Twillingate and later to Edwin Duder in the middle and later 1800's.

The first Andrew Pearce in the following eight years of his life at Twillingate took a great interest in the life of St Peter's Anglican Church there and, on his death in 1841, the congregation put up a marble tablet on the church wall in memory of him.

There are, too, references to a number of "Colbournes" in Twillingate. Andrew Pearce in Poole used to spell John Colborne's name in this way, but we do not really know what happened to the Colbornes of Sturminster after the bankruptcy in 1834 or whether the Colbournes of Twillingate were connected with them. Nor, unfortunately, do we know the house of the once well-off William Colborne, the "old gentleman", who probably should have sold his business when he retired in 1821 if he was to have retained the bulk of his fortune, much of which he left tied up in the ships, fishing installations and credit in the hands of his planters in Newfoundland.

Of the proud sailing ships of the Colbornes which for decades sailed in and out of the port of Poole – the *Thomas and Rebecca*, the *Dorset*, the *Dispatch*, the *Enterprise*, the *Elizabeth*, the *Commerce*, the *Dove* and the *Seal* – we have only their distinguishing ship's pennants to remind us of them, plus the house-flag of the Colbornes of Sturminster and Poole.

The Arms of Poole
1563

Poole Corporation Flag

The Rectory of St James
and its Rectors

The Rectory of St James was called "the parsonage house" for all its early life, even after the present building was erected by the merchants of the Poole Corporation in 1786. To the burgesses who formed the Poole Corporation all matters affecting the interests of Poole should be in their hands as part and parcel of their rightful administration of the town which they had made. Therefore it would have been an early ambition of the merchants to wrest the ownership of the church in Poole from the Lord of the Manor in the same way as they had obtained rights to trade in the port, pasture their cattle on common land, hold fairs in the town and enjoy many other privileges, a process which started with the concessions made by the Lord of the Manor in 1248 in the Longespee Charter.

Any such early ambitions in regard to the church, however, had been pre-empted by the Lord of the Manor having given away his original ownership of the church at Canford and its chapel of St James at Poole. The very early Lords of the Manor had, by a series of grants, given the churches with their attendant rights to the Augustinian monks (the Black Monks) of Bradenstoke in Wiltshire, a priory which the devout son of the very first Norman Lord of the Manor of Cheneford (as Canford was earlier called) had founded in 1142.

While the churches were owned and administered by the Prior of Bradenstoke it was not possible for the Poole merchants to have any sway in the Prior's appointment of the priests in charge of the chapel at Poole. The Prior of Bradenstoke did, however, in his appointment of the priests in Poole, effectively separate the Poole church from the Canford one, and it was he who attached to Poole the tithes of Parkstone and Longfleet to give it financial support. This position continued for nearly 400 years except that gradually the chapel at Poole was extended until it finally became a large church. Two aisles were added to the original building in this period, first on the south side and then, around 1500, James Haviland and his wife Helene paid for a second, narrower aisle to be added on the north side. In addition, four altars were established in the church, one of them dedicated to the Poole fraternity of St George. The Mayor of Poole was always the head of this ancient local fraternity, and it was he who appointed the special priest for service at this altar. (The Corporation in 1586 even purchased back from the Queen the fraternity's old possessions which had been seized in Edward VI's reign: they paid £21 14s 2d. for them.)

In 1539, however, everything was drastically changed by Henry VIII's dissolution of the monasteries. In that year William Snow, the last Prior of Bradenstoke, accepted an appointment as Dean of Bristol and a pension of £60 a year, and surrendered his monastery, its lands and possessions. There is some doubt whether the Prior had foreseen the loss of the Priory's possessions and sold the Poole church and its rights to the chaplain William Birte, or whether he had in the ordinary course of his adminstration appointed William Birte to be the priest in charge at Poole.

Whatever doubt there remains on this score, though, there is no doubt as to what happened to them thereafter: the churches at Canford and Poole were escheated to the King. Then, by the King's ownership they became "Royal Peculiars", churches whose administration was not subject to the usual control and discipline of the Bishops' Courts and whose owners and priests thereafter were answerable only to the King himself.

No dramatic changes were made in the management of the Poole church immediately following the King's acquisition. William Birte continued as the chaplain at Poole and was allowed to continue his ministry until his death in 1547, the same year as Henry VIII himself died. It was therefore Edward VI who took action in regard to the monarch's new possession, and he decided to lease out his rights over the church at Poole. In the same year as he succeeded to the throne he leased "the church and rectory of Poole, with all its appurtenances; and all tithes, oblations, obventions, pensions, portions, and all other possessions, hereditaments, revenues and profits whatsoever" to John Hannam of Wimborne. The lease was for 21 years at an annual rent of £12.

Under the powers of his lease John Hannam appointed Thomas Hancock, an "earnest preacher in the south-west parts . . . whose mouth had been stopped by a strict inhibition from preaching in the former King's reign" because of his strong Protestant views. He was a brave man and got himself into many conflicts. In a sermon at Southampton, for instance, he took it upon himself to criticise the church's vicar for holding mass in his church. The vicar of the church, no less brave than Thomas Hancock, promptly stood up and announced "Mr Hancock, you have done well unto now; and now you have played an ill cow's part which, when she hath given a good mess of milk, overthroweth all with her foot, and so all is lost" and, says the old account, the vicar "got him out of church"!

Nearer at home Thomas Hancock was no less outspoken in his beliefs. Preaching in the old St James in 1545 on his favourite subjects of idolatry and covetousness he offended the Mayor, "olde Thomas Whyghtt, a great ryche marchantt" (as Hancock himself described him) so much that Thomas Whyte marched out of church crying, "Come from hym, good people. He came from the divell and teachest you divilish doctrines". Later that year, on All Saints' Day, Thomas Whyte and John Northerell, a previous Mayor of Poole, went to St James and, when Thomas Hancock refused their demands to celebrate mass, they pushed him into the vestry and locked him in. But they failed in their purpose, for they still had no priest to celebrate mass.

Eight years later Mary was on the throne and since she was hostile to reform, Thomas Whyte and John Northerell when he was Mayor again, were encouraged to have another try. They got a priest to come over from France and built an altar in St James so that mass could be celebrated, but once again they were foiled by the Rector who promptly had the altar pulled down. Then, when Thomas Whyte had an altar erected in his own house and a bell erected on the eaves of his house to call the faithful to mass, he was cheated in his hoped-for publicity by the ringing of the bell. When the recently appointed bell-ringer, John Craddock, put his hand out of the window to ring the bell for mass there was a supporter of the Rector standing outside who quietly told John Craddock that if he put his hand out of the window once more his arm would be shot at, "so thatte he sholld not pull in his hand agayne with ease"! Thomas Whyte then retired from Poole to his house of Fiddleford Mill, Sturminster Newton (which still exists and which, perhaps, is the first of Poole merchants' mansions) where he died in 1555, and there were no further efforts to celebrate the Roman Catholic mass at St James.

Hancock was among the priests who were specifically exempted from the Queen's general pardon and, from that moment, he was in danger of immediate arrest. He thereupon fled to France, and it was not safe for him to return to England until Elizabeth had come to the throne. Meanwhile events in Poole had not stayed still. Now that the lease of the church was in private hands the Corporation could consider how they could themselves acquire it and their efforts seemed finally to succeed when, before the end of the term granted to John Hannam, he surrendered the lease to Matthew Haviland. The Haviland family were prominent merchants in the Corporation of Poole; in fact, Richard Haviland had previously appointed a priest to serve one of the four altars in St James, and no less than five different Havilands had been Mayor of Poole totalling 11 years between them, and it seems more than likely that Matthew Haviland was acting as the nominee of the merchants in taking over John Hannam's lease, especially as, a few years later, he transferred it formally to the "mayor, bailiffs, burgesses and commonalty of Poole".

Any arrangements that there might have been between Matthew Haviland and the Corporation were not one-sided for Matthew Haviland was a "clerk" and it was he himself who took on the duties of chaplain at Poole. But, whatever feelings of gratitude the merchants may have first felt towards Matthew Haviland in his being their instrument in obtaining the control of the church, such feelings wore thin as his ministry proceeded. Finally, they decided that his preaching was "obnoxious", and that he would have to go.

Probably because of lingering gratitude to him for what he had done, the merchants decided that the most pleasant way of getting rid of Matthew Haviland was to promote him. They therefore bought from the chapter of Wells Cathedral the right to make the next presentation of the vicar at Martock in Somerset. They then persuaded the Vicar of Martock to retire and offered the position to Matthew Haviland. We do not know whether these arrangements were made with Matthew Haviland's connivance or not but, when the position at Martock was offered to Matthew Haviland, he refused it. The merchants' reaction was predictable: they held him to the resignation which they had extracted from him and appointed a new rector, Robert Ryckman, in his place. However, as Matthew Haviland appears soon afterwards as Vicar of Bloxworth, it seems that he was quite able to look after his own interests.

Robert Ryckman, the first rector to be appointed by the Corporation, stayed nine years in Poole before resigning in 1579, but the two following appointments by the Corporation first of Robert Forsey and then of Richard Marcam, seem to have been less successful, for both of them resigned within a year of their appointment.

We can only speculate as to whether the condition of the accommodation which was afforded the rectors of Poole had anything to do with these early resignations, but it is significant that on the appointment of William Hiley in 1582, the Corporation built a new parsonage house for him and William Hiley remained as Rector of Poole for the rest of his life. In fact the 29 years of William Hiley's rectorship of Poole was a most significant period in national and religious history. It was during his curacy that the Warbarrow Beacons were lit to signify the approach of the Spanish Armada and, says H Lawrence Phillips in his *Poole Church and its Rectors*, Hiley saw depart from Poole "*The Castell of Comforte, The Grace of Gode, The Stetts*, the *Bounauenter* and many besides", to join in the fray. It was, too, William Hiley, as Rector of Poole, who received the very first copy of the authorised version of the Bible for use in St James.

The Poole Corporation still only had the leasehold of the rights over the church and in 1584, when the lease was coming to an end, the Corporation made an order that anyone taking goods out of Poole overseas should pay to the Mayor 4d. in the £ of the cost of the freight for the "preacher of God's word within the town". Then, when they applied for the renewal of their lease they were, too, at pains to point out to the Queen's advisors how well they had carried out their duties. They had provided "a sufficient curate or preacher", and the profit of their ownership had "little surmounted" Her Majesty's yearly rent. They had, moreover, rebuilt the parsonage house. Robert Freke was sent to Poole to check up on their claims, and the Augmentation Officer was later able to report, "I am informed by Robert Freke, gent., her majesty's surveyor of the said countie, that they have (to their great charge) newe buylded the p'sonage howse there, wch was in great decaye".

It is doubtful, despite the "great charge" to the merchants, whether this parsonage house could in any sense be called a mansion, but it was sufficient to persuade Queen Elizabeth not to call for the usual "fine" on the renewal of their lease of the church.

The Corporation continued as lessees for many years, but, however dynamically they dealt with the administration of church matters, their hold was still tenuous in that they were merely tenants of the monarch of their rights. There was always the doubt as to the lease's renewal when it fell in at the expiry of each term. But, however foreseeing the merchants were, they had probably not reckoned on the monarch unilaterally abrogating their lease while it was still current: but that is what happened.

In 1606 James I had granted the Corporation a further lease of the church at Poole with its appurtenant rights and duties; this time for a period of 40 years at a rental of £12 16s. 0d. While this lease was still current, however, Charles I gave the church, the rectory, the advowson (the right to appoint the priest) and its tithes to his friend, the Countess of Anglesea, subject to her paying him the same sum as his father had previously let the rights to the Corporation.

It is not difficult to imagine the indignation of the Poole merchants when they heard that the King had abrogated their lease, nor is it difficult to believe that this was at least a factor in the town's support of the Parliamentary forces a few years later when the King could have done with all the support he could have got.

However, the Countess of Anglesea required quick money to satisfy her husband's creditors rather than a doubtful investment in church rights. Within a month of receiving her royal gift she had found a willing purchaser in Thomas Smithby of London who paid her £256 for the freehold of the church and its rights and this purchase by Thomas Smithby meant that the real and effective ownership was at last in private hands.

Robert Smithby was, though, no nominee purchaser of the rights as Matthew Haviland had probably been. For the ensuing 14 years he used his new powers over the Poole church. In fact he made no less than four consecutive appointments to the chaplaincy of the church.

The last of his appointments was that of John Hadderley in 1647 – the year when Cromwell's forces first arrested Charles I. Whether Mr Smithby made his appointment early in 1647, before Charles's arrest that year, or after his escape is not clear. It is more likely that it was after his escape, for the new Rector of Poole was a King's man, a great supporter of the King's cause which, of course, was irretrievably lost in 1649 when the King was executed. It was, too, hardly likely that the rector's views would have been to the liking of the merchants or most of Poole's population, for Poole was predominantly a pro-Parliamentary town.

It was therefore not long after Cromwell came into power that John Hadderley was declared ousted from his living at Poole by an order from Cromwell. He was arrested at the Rectory and imprisoned in the Poole gaol in Fish Street under the meeting room of the Corporation, but seems to have escaped or been freed on repentance for, when he died in 1699, he was minister of a dissenting church in Salisbury.

Even prior to this disgrace of his protégé in Poole Mr Smithby had been in trouble for, it seemed, he had taken all the revenues to which the church was entitled without providing a reasonable allowance for the priest. In 1648 the House of Commons referred the case of Mr Smithby and the church at Poole to the "Committee for Plundered Ministers" with an instruction to send for Mr Smithby to make sure that he made a "competent allowance to a preaching minister in the said Parish".

Mr Smithby must have been embarrassed by the sudden turn of events with his appointee, John Hadderley languishing in gaol. His apprehensions were probably heightened by the fact that Poole had then been designated as a garrison town by Cromwell's army, and any mistaken appointment would soon be brought to official notice.

Such fears were not ones which the old burgesses of Poole would harbour. They were not the kind of men to let fears inhibit their actions, and this seemed a wonderful chance for them finally to seize hold of the freehold of the church. In fact, had the burgesses been at all timorous, they might well have wondered at that time whether the powers and privileges, all directly granted by the monarch, would not themselves have been completely nullified on Charles's execution and the demise of all the monarch's powers.

If the burgesses had any such apprehensions they did not show them. They saw the occasion as a good chance to get the freehold rights of the church into their own hands at a bargain price. Twelve of them contributed various sums to add up to £100 which they offered to Mr Smithby for the freehold of the church and its rights, and Mr Smithby seems to have been only too happy to come to a quick agreement.

For their £100 the Mayor and 11 of his brother burgesses, all merchants of Poole, bought "all that Rectory and Church of Poole with all its Rights, members and appurtenances and all houses, barnes, stables, pedgeon houses, yards, Gardens, Orchard, Glebe lands, the Tenths of Corne, grayne and Hay, Wool, Flax, Hemp and also all tenths of fish and fowle and all other tithes and tenths as well as great as Small and all offerings, Revenues, Fruits, profitts and Hereditaments whatsoever in Poole aforesaid and elsewhere in the County of Dorset . . .".

The Mayor, magistrates and burgesses were to receive the profits of the transaction after the first six years during which the 12 trustees intended to repay themselves their original contributions and the Corporation was to be able to dispose of the future income as they thought fit. The trustees undertook to ratify all bargains made by the Corporation and were to ensure their own continued existence by electing new trustees from time to time so that their numbers never fell below seven.

The "free farm rent" of £12 16s. 0d. a year which the Countess of Anglesea had agreed to pay to the King was the only charge on the Corporation's ownership, a payment which was regularly made by them for the rest of their long ownership of the church.

This period, when Thomas Smithby was awaiting on events and negotiating the sale of the church to the Corporation, was also the time when other churches were in similar straits with their vicars dispossessed, and Parliament allowed marriages to take place other than in a church. They allowed marriages to be made before Justices of the Peace. In this period marriages were "proclaimed", and one of the first of such marriages ended with an entry in St James register of 17th June 1658 which read: "John Hann, late of Mawgan, in Connoll, now of Wimborne, gent., and Mary Arrendell, daughter of Thomas Arrendell, gent., deceased, was lawfully published in ye Markett Place, and no objection to the contrarie".

The title page of the book published by Samuel Hardy in 1684, two years after he had left Poole, but still having a section especially addressed to his old congregation.

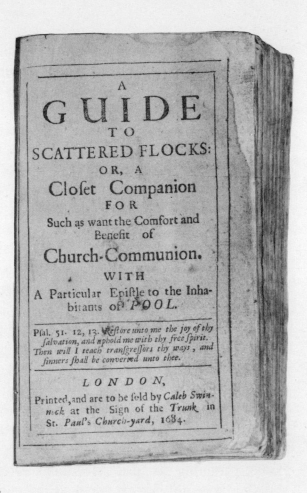

A
GUIDE
TO
SCATTERED FLOCKS:
OR, A
Closet Companion
FOR
Such as want the Comfort and Benefit of
Church-Communion.
WITH
A Particular Epistle to the Inhabitants of *POOL*.

Psal. 51. 12, 13. *Restore unto me the joy of thy salvation, and uphold me with thy free spirit. Then will I teach transgressors thy ways, and sinners shall be converted unto thee.*

LONDON,
Printed, and are to be sold by *Caleb Swinnock* at the Sign of the *Trunk* in St. *Paul's Church-yard*, 1684.

A
SERMON
PREACHED
Before the Mayor, Aldermen, and Burgesses of the Town and County of *Poole* in *Dorsetshire*, on Friday the 20th Day of *September*, 1700, immediately before the Electing a Mayor, and other Officers for the following Year.

By *WILLIAM CHURCHEY*, M. A.
And Minister of the Parish-Church of St. *James's*, within the said Town and County.

Prov. 23. 3. *He that ruleth over Men must be just, ruling in the fear of God.*

LONDON;
Printed by *J. D.* for the Author, MDCCI.

The Burgesses might nominate the Rector but, once elected, they were then part of his flock. William Churchey's sermon on the day before the election of the Mayor and other Corporate officers in 1700 was taken by him to remind them of their duties to society and the effect of their decisions on the well-being of the town. Good magistrates serving Justice would lead to a happy people and God would "bless our ships, and bless our men; He would send us good success and happy voyages. . . " Some of the Burgesses "could hardly give it a Hearing and others were so much offended at it, that they have fearce spoken to the author since." He had it printed in April, 1701, in London.

157

But the absence of a rector in the garrison town of Poole gave rise to other difficulties, and it was typical of the merchants to become involved in an argument about the appointment of the rector even before the legal formalities of their purchase had been completed.

With the delay in the appointment of the rector after the ousting of John Hadderley, Colonel Rede, Cromwell's military governor of Poole, became concerned about the absence of a rector. He later claimed that, as the Mayor had not procured a preacher to take the Thanksgiving Day service, he had been driven to take matters into his own hands. Whatever the reason, it was a fact that Colonel Rede had asked a Mr Gardiner to come to St James to conduct the Thanksgiving Service.

Here was a cause on which all Poole men could agree, churchmen and Corporation. As a matter of principle they were having no rector of their church appointed by a military governor whoever he might represent. One hundred and thirty-two churchmen signed a "humble petition of the godly engaged party in the town" to the Mayor protesting against the Governor's action. The Corporation lent their full support to the petition, adding their own condemnation of the Governor's action. The Mayor soon had both memorials in the hands of the Governor and Mr Gardiner had soon left the town, though his only fault was that he had appeared to have been foisted on the town. The Corporation soon afterwards appointed their own rector, Thomas Thackham.

At the restoration in 1660 the Rev Thackham kept his position as Rector of Poole, probably because the Poole church was a "Royal Peculiar" and the rector was therefore not susceptible to dismissal by the Bishop's Court. It was about this time that Poole began to divide its religious life between St James and various dissenting religions for, although George Fox, the Quaker, had visited Poole previously, it was not until 1672 that the first licence was taken out by a dissenting minister. The licence was given to William Minty, a mercer in Poole, who held services in Mr Aire's malthouse. (Needless to say, the Corporation promptly ejected Mr Minty from his burgesship of Poole for so doing.)

It was therefore not until the death of Thomas Thackham in 1667 that the Corporation was called upon to make its first considered choice of a new rector. The burgesses must have known when they chose Samuel Hardy to be the Rector of Poole that he really was a Presbyterian, for he had been vicar at nearby Charminster. His ministry had only been able to continue there because that church also was a Royal Peculiar and thus protected from the Bishop. He had even been sent down from Oxford for refusing the oaths then required to be awarded the degree of a Master of Arts. The result was that for the first 15 years the church under the aegis of the Corporation had a Rector who never wore a surplice, read only those parts of the prayer book which he happened to approve, and generally ran the church as though it was a Presbyterian chapel!

For all that Samuel Hardy was a popular minister and came to have a considerable influence in Poole. At Charminster the Trenchard family had given him great support so that when Thomas Trenchard put himself forward as a candidate in

158

Poole for election to Parliament in 1671 it was Samuel Hardy's support which was said to have carried the day against his Parliamentary opponent, the son of the Lord Chancellor, the Earl of Shaftesbury. But Samuel Hardy's popularity was not universal. He was a particular thorn in the flesh of the assize juries at Dorchester. "This hired non-conformist preacher", they complained, "was using St James Church as a conventicle" to which "multitudes of His Majesty's disaffected subjects within the County do constantly resort". Most of the rest of Dorset at the time were royalist and resented that the town's privileges of autonomy allowed the Rector in Poole to be protected from the county's jurisdiction.

However, the assize juries had the best of the argument in the end. In 1681 the grand jury at Dorchester had found sufficient evidence for them to make a presentment to the assize judge to the effect that Hardy's activities were "a great hinderance to the execution of the laws both civil and ecclesiastical", and the jury asked the judge to beseech the King "in his princely wisdom to think of some expedient for the redress thereof".

Whether the burgesses really agreed with the jury or whether they feared for their future ownership of the church if the judge's request had reached the King first we shall never know, but Allen Skutt and other Poole burgesses promptly made their own petition to the King suggesting that Mr Hardy should be removed from office. A commission was appointed to inquire into the facts, and the King signed a decree on 3rd August 1682 ousting Mr Hardy from his rectorship at Poole. His non-conformist ministry in Poole had lasted nearly 15 years.

On the dismissal of Samuel Hardy, the Corporation appointed Robert Howson as Rector, but he resigned after three years in office and was succeeded by John Russell. This was in the same year as James II became King and the Rector was immediately in the thick of the religious controversies of the time.

Poole had always been predominantly Protestant. The Duke of Monmouth had visited Poole with his father Charles II some years previously and was conscious of there being support for him in Poole but, happily for the peace of Poole, he landed at Lyme Regis rather than at Poole to lead what he hoped would be a successful insurrection against James II. It was, too, lucky for Poole that Samuel Hardy was then at Newbury and not still Rector of Poole, for there is little doubt that he and his followers would have tried, like some of the family of Trenchards, his old patrons at Charminster, who were then living at Lytchett House, to have given practical support to "King Monmouth". Thomas Trenchard, whom Hardy had helped win one of Poole's two seats in Parliament, had died in 1684 but his place had been taken by Henry Trenchard. On the other hand Thomas Chaffin, the other Member of Parliament from Poole, supported the King against Monmouth and even led a troop of soldiers in the King's support and was involved in the Battle of Sedgemoor when Monmouth's irregular soldiers were defeated.

When Monmouth had got as far as Frome in his flight from Sedgemoor he decided to go to Poole "a little seaport not far off, where we were to seize ship and set sail for Holland again, leaving the infantry to the mercy of the country". Happily for Poole, Monmouth changed his mind and moved from Frome towards the New Forest. When this became known it fell to the lot of Poole's ex-Recorder, Antony Ettricke, to sign the committal warrant authorising Monmouth's arrest. The Duke was arrested on the road from Horton to Ringwood and was executed at Tower Hill a few days later.

James II's success encouraged him to issue his Declaration of Indulgences to bring relief to the Catholics and, when the bishops and clergy refused to read out the declaration from their pulpits, the King had the bishops indicted with the serious criminal offence of seditious libel.

The Rector's lot in Poole at the time must have been a most difficult one for the church was deeply involved in the national controversies. Many Poole men must have been involved in open opposition to the King for, although the only record of the times in Poole seems to be a note to the Mayor on how to dispose of the quarters, hands and feet of rebels hanged in Poole, it is sufficient to indicate the extent of the troubles surrounding the new Rector even though self-preservation dictated that Poole's troubles went unrecorded. It would have been a brave but foolhardy man who would have kept records then with such reminders as the gruesome remains of hanged men suspended on poles and spikes at Upper Lytchett.

Arising in the period of the Commonwealth, when there was no King to receive the Corporations' annual payment of £12 16s. 0d., it had been left to the Recorder of the borough to allocate the amount to charity. The Recorder of Poole at the time was Antony Ettricke who lived at Holt Lodge near Wimborne and, to quote Sydenham, he "towards his latter days grew humorsome and phlegmatic". In fact it was he who, in one of his "fits of spleen against the people of Wimborne", swore that he would be buried "neither in the church nor out of their church, neither above the ground nor below it". Later he even obtained the church's permission to comply with his vow of not having his coffin either in or out of the church by having it put within the thickness of the wall of the church and, to comply with having it neither above nor below the ground, he had it placed level with the adjoining pavement.

He was buried in accordance with his wishes in 1703 and in his will he stipulated how the £12 16s. 0d. rental payable by the Corporation should be paid. The first £1 each year was to be payable to the churchwardens of Wimborne Minster for the purpose of keeping his coffin in a state of good preservation. He was "buried" as he directed, and his coffin was placed in the wall of the Minster, partly raised from the ground, painted with its coat of arms and clamped together with iron bands. The eccentric Recorder left a further £2 a year to the fellows of Queen's College, Oxford, "to be spent in wine and tobacco on the 5th November each year".

The balance of the Corporation's rent charge of £9 16s. 0d. a year was disposed of more conventionally by giving it to the poor of St Margaret's Hospital, Wimborne. (These payments were queried many times by curious burgesses over the following 150 years or so, as they saw these surprising payments in the Corporation's accounts!)

A view of the old Church of St James which was demolished in 1819.

Antony Ettricke's coffin — "neither in the Church nor out of their Church, neither above the ground nor below it."

The Unitarian Meeting House was in Hill Street.
To the left of the photograph was the Green Market and further to the left was the old
Police Station, Market Place and the Guildhall.

'The Independent Chapel', Poole.

162

However, there were other provisions of the Corporation's lease which were not so meticulously observed. In 1692, on the early death of the Rector, James Hanne, who had followed John Russell on his resignation in 1691, it was found that Moses Durell was the only survivor of the original trustees of the 1650 deed. They had failed to comply with the provision to appoint new trustees to ensure that there were never less than seven.

It is curious that this problem had not been foreseen when James Hanne had been appointed Rector only the year before. But, to overcome any further problems the Corporation repaid Moses Durell the sum of £44 12s. 0d. which he had spent on repairs to the rectory and church, and he conveyed the church, its property and rights to Shadrach Beale the Mayor, and 11 other burgesses who were to hold the premises in trust for the Corporation.

The new deed of conveyance of 1692, designed to settle all matters of doubt, suffered from misunderstandings and quarrels from the very next appointment of a rector.

William Churchey, who had been Rector from 1692 died in 1702. The Corporation thereupon had a meeting at which it was resolved to appoint Daniel Hyde as the town's rector. Their appointment was accepted by the Rev William Guise, the official of the exempt jurisdiction of Great Canford, as an appropriate appointment made by the Corporation under the 1692 deed. Meanwhile the incoming Mayor, Sir William Phippard who had also been Mayor previously, with William Jolliffe MP for Poole joined Moses Durell, the original conveyer of the church and some of the new trustees of the 1692 deed to claim that the right to electing the new rector belonged to the trustees named in the deed and not of the whole body of the burgesses of the Corporation. Some of them therefore met to assert these rights and elected Richard Mayo as the new Rector of Poole, calling themselves "the proprietors of the Rectory Impropriate of Poole". They then issued a writ in the High Court of Delegates which was served on Rev Guise, the official of Great Canford, and Daniel Hyde, the rector elected by the burgesses. They claimed rectification of the "unlawful act of the Burgesses" in electing Daniel Hyde as rector and the official for accepting this election. The court set up a commission to examine witnesses in Poole and to report back to the court. But the case dragged on for three years and caused a great deal of friction among the burgesses as well as among the congregation of the church. Many, including Moses Durell himself as well as two others of the original 12 trustees named in the 1692 deed, left St James altogether in this period and joined the Hill Street chapel.

With this having happened the petitioners lost interest in the church and its quarrels and dropped their case but by this time Daniel Hyde, like many of his successors, must have felt that it was quite impossible for him to conduct a success-ful ministry in the turbulent waters of Poole's acrimonious arguments and the commission's long inquiries among the parishioners: he resigned to help bring the sorry business to an end.

The subsequent election of John Conant was clear. It was by the burgesses at a recorded meeting at the Guildhall in Fish Street. Sir William Phippard, who surprisingly had been elected Mayor in two of the three years when he was named as the principal appellant against the Corporation's choice of the previous rector, was this time a supporter of John Conant, the successful applicant. The younger burgesses, John Lester, Peter Jolliffe, William Williams, Will Williams and John Wills supported a Mr Shorthose. The burgesses therefore took a vote and John Conant was voted the new rector by 15 votes to five. Henry Andress and Samuel Baker, two other applicants, did not get a single vote between them. The voting does show clearly, though, that it was the whole of the burgesses attending the meeting who were allowed to vote and it was certainly not only the 12 trustees named in the deed.

There was then peace for some years for John Conant was rector for 15 years and then, in 1720, the Corporation appointed Christopher Derby, the schoolmaster, to be Rector. These were the times when smuggling was so rife that even the Poole Corporation petitioned Parliament to remedy it as there was "a great decay of their home manufactures by reason of the great quantities of goods run". When the Government later did something to stop the "free traders" and it was found how many notable citizens were being incommoded by the measures, the Corporation then petitioned Parliament that the measures being taken were too rigorous and should be taken with less repression! H Lawrence Phillips, a later Rector of Poole, wrote that this appointment of a schoolmaster as rector, tallied with the needs of the times for a schoolmaster rector!

Christopher Derby was followed in 1734 by his brother Richard who was also vicar of Hilton and he, like his brother, was universally accepted by the burgesses and inhabitants and St James extended its interlude of peace up to 1748.

On Richard Derby's death in that year, however, peace came to an end. There were then several contenders for the vacant living and, unfortunately for the peace of the church, the two leading contenders both had relatives who were burgesses of Poole, both of whom pressed their relatives' claims with the burgesses' usual wholeheartedness. Mr John Culme was one of the applicants and he was the brother-in-law of Joseph Bowles, a leading burgess who was to be Mayor a couple of years afterwards. The other main contender, George Henning, was the son of another leading burgess, Robert Henning, who had been Mayor of Poole for three consecutive years a few years previously.

The Corporation had adopted the practice of inviting the various applicants to preach a "probationary sermon" in St James to help them decide who should be their new rector. Although this seemed a sensible procedure it did have the disadvantage of prolonging the process of selection and thereby giving more time for trouble to brew up.

On this occasion, as in all others, the period of the vacancy and the preaching of the probationary sermons was filled by the candidates in canvassing. The supporters of the various candidates for the rectorship, often supported by their legal adviser to introduce the candidate and support his case, walked round the town calling on the burgesses, and sometimes the ordinary inhabitants, canvassing for their votes.

In the case of the choice between John Culme and George Henning in 1748 the votes of ordinary inhabitants of Poole who attended the old Guildhall were taken. This process was said to be correct by Robert Henning, a former Mayor of considerable standing in the town, and his son, George Henning, was declared elected the new Rector of Poole despite "a great bustle and uproar at the time of such election" as a witness later put it. George Henning was installed rector and took the services at St James for the following two or three weeks.

The election of a rector in Poole, however, still needed the licence of the Official of the Church of Great Canford, and the Corporation were not slow to put in a caveat with the Official objecting to the licensing of George Henning as Rector of Poole.

Meanwhile a further election was held at the Old Guildhall in Fish Street at which only the burgesses were allowed to vote. The then Mayor of Poole, John Masters, was probably the leading figure in both the church and the Corporation. Peter Jolliffe said later that he thought that the Corporation or the inhabitants would have supported whichever of the candidates he had recommended, such was his standing in the town. The burgesses certainly seem to have done so that day for they elected John Culme as the Rector. John Tilsed remembered the event quite vividly even 50 years later, for he said everybody in the Guildhall, burgesses and public alike, gave "huzzars or shouts" at Culme's election and he remembered that there was a crowd assembled round the Guildhall in Fish Street to welcome the victorious Rector.

But, although Robert Henning thereby lost the election of his son as Poole's Rector, his assertions as to who might vote at the election of rectors were believed by many. They still put this point to the registrar of Great Canford and, before he licensed John Culme in August 1748, he took the opinion of Sir Dudley Ryder a leading ecclesiastical lawyer, as to whether the right of election lay in the Burgesses alone or in the inhabitants at large. Sir Dudley's view was that it lay solely with the Corporation and John Culme was duly licensed as Poole's next rector, even though he was also vicar of Old Cleeve in Somerset and the rector of More Critchell in Dorset.

John Culme died in office in 1755 and it might have been expected that the question of the right of election had now been finally settled. The tenacious Poole inhabitants, however, took the loss of one battle only as a lesson in how to win the next one. By 1755, too, the uniting force of John Masters's personality had gone for he had died in London when on business there in June of that year.

In 1755 the same procedure of candidates being asked to take services and preach probationary sermons was again adopted. Although this was a period of the church's decadence and loss of power and with deistical and unitarian views becoming prevalent, as Poole was only too well aware, the church of St James was still filled to its capacity at the services in the church. In fact the main controversies in the church during John Culme's ministry seemed to revolve round the question of the allocation of pews, such was the demand for them. Thomas Dean, for instance, erected his own pew in the church in 1751 and the church entry read "The seat between Mr Christopher Jolliffe's seat and Mr Henry Price's seat was erected by Thomas Dean, and is for himself, his wife and children and their families, and none else, 26 May 1751".

With this interest in the church, and the only rates paid by the inhabitants being paid through the parish collectors, the inhabitants felt they had good cause to be involved directly in the election of their rector rather than leaving it merely to the burgesses, many of whom were now nonconformists in any case.

Having heard the probationary sermons preached in church by the candidates for the rectorship in 1755, the congregation of the church were in no doubt as to which of the candidates should then be elected rector. It was a clear, and nearly unanimous decision of those attending the services that Mr William Nairn was their man, for he was an excellent preacher. In fact, some of the burgesses themselves, notably Peter Jolliffe, were also entirely convinced. On the other hand, George Tito, the Mayor, together with Peter Jolliffe's uncle, William Jolliffe, and a majority of the burgesses favoured Mr Basket.

The Corporation had successfully asserted its rights at the election of Mr Culme. The registrar, it had been established, would only license the preacher of the Corporation's choice as the Rector of Poole. George Tito, the Mayor, called a meeting of the burgesses and invited Mr Basket to come down from Wiltshire to stay with him. The two walked down to the Guildhall together, the Mayor having taken the precaution of having the church keys in his pocket and the meeting went according to the Mayor's plan. The burgesses duly elected Mr Basket as their new rector.

Unfortunately for Mr Basket, however, the worshippers of St James had thought little of the probationary sermon which Mr Basket had preached in the church. He had a low voice and in the crowded church he had been inaudible to many of them. They could not stomach the thought of him being made their rector.

Thomas Casely, one of the churchwardens, took the lead on behalf of the congregation. He got the vestry clerk, Richard Corpe, who was also the local schoolmaster, to call a meeting in the church at the same time as the burgesses were meeting in Fish Street. The crowded vestry meeting decided that their views should hold sway in the election of a rector and that all those then paying scot and lot (which technically should have, they thought, entitled them to burgesship of the town), should have a vote. If such a vote was taken it was clear, they decided, that it would be overwhelmingly in favour of Mr Nairn. They even decided that Mr Basket was a "very unfit man" to be their rector. They therefore proceeded to elect Mr Nairn as their rector.

Meanwhile at the Guildhall the burgesses having duly elected Mr Basket, walked down together with their new rector to the church to put him formally into possession of it.

They had not reckoned on the lengths to which Thomas Casely and his friends would go. They had found a way into the church through the belfry door for their meeting. Then, when the mayor and burgesses arrived at the church for the formal ceremony of Mr Basket taking possession of the church, they found the mayor's key was of little avail against the barred doors of the church. New locks had been fixed to the door and large bars placed across the inside.

Inside the church, when the Mayor and the burgesses arrived, Mr Casely was formally giving possession of the church to the vestry's newly-elected rector, Mr Nairn. They led Mr Nairn solemnly to the pulpit where they "presented him to the church" and "put him in possession of the desk" after which the baffled and infuriated burgesses outside the church had the mortification of hearing the new "rector" tolling the big bell of the church as the last rite of his having completed his taking over the possession and care of the church.

This satisfactorily completed, Mr Casely and his colleagues opened the vestry door and, to quote an eye-witness, "there was a great bustle" between the vestry and the burgesses who had been cooling their heels but not their tempers outside the church. Some of the irate burgesses, never loth to accept new powers, told Casely that he would be excommunicated, while others threatened him and his friends with a law suit for having desecrated the church "in performing mock and illegal solemnities".

In no way discountenanced Casely turned the new solid locks of the vestry door against the burgesses and the bewildered Mr Basket who had, he thought, been Rector of Poole for the last half hour. Mr Casely and his colleagues then promptly started a collection to defray the costs of the threatened law suit, for they knew enough of the burgesses' character to have little hope that they would accept their *fait accompli* without a fight.

The following Sunday Mr Basket arrived at the church to find Mr Nairn already esconced in church with Mr Casely guarding the door. Mr Basket felt there was little alternative but to retreat from the church where the service proceeded under the conduct of Mr Nairn, as it did on subsequent Sundays.

The rebel churchgoers all helped to retain their own rector in possession. The church was kept locked till Mr Nairn arrived and "after the Duty, proper persons" were appointed from the congregation to see the people out of church and to secure it until the next service.

The burgesses meanwhile were not idle. They had entered a caveat at the registry against the issue of any licence to Mr Nairn and they got their new rector and his attorney to enter a writ against Mr Nairn, Mr Casely and Mr Corpe and others. This sort of situation was not new to the burgesses and, from the precedent of previous elections, they must have felt confident that the law was on their side. But they had not reckoned on two things. The first surprising fact was that both Mr Basket and Mr Nairn had the same attorney, a Mr Weston of Ringwood. It was the second fact, however, which was the fatal flaw: their rector turned out to be, in the scathing words of George Tito, the Mayor, a "timid man". Mr Basket, in fact, was not well off and had a large family and, as the Mayor later told his daughter, "Mr Basket had no stomach for a law suit". Though it seems surprising to us that Mr Weston could feel he could properly advise both contestants, he was at least in a good position to compromise the action. He probably felt that it would have been impossible for Mr Basket ever to have been a successful rector of Poole after all that had happened. Whatever happened behind the scenes, the upshot of it all was that Mr Nairn agreed to pay the £40 costs which Mr Basket had so far incurred with Mr Weston as well as his own costs, and Mr Basket thereupon resigned from his position as rector of the church he had only been in once, and then to preach a probationary sermon! Thus the solicitor got his costs from both sides and Mr Nairn was left as *de facto* Rector of Poole.

The Mayor and burgesses were not ones to capitulate readily. Perhaps they took their anger and frustration out on their cowardly candidate, for Mrs Elizabeth Brice, the daughter of the Mayor probably understated the vehemence of her father when she says that he had said Mr Basket was a timid man and had no stomach for a fight. Whatever was said there was, unfortunately, only one thing to be done, and that was for the Corporation then to force themselves to accept the vestry's choice. They elected Mr Nairn as Rector of St James and withdrew their caveat at the Canford Registry.

Mr Nairn held the office of Rector of Poole for 12 years till his death in 1767. By this time, of course, the dispute over the powers of the inhabitants or vestry to take part in the election of the rector were now even more in doubt following the success of the churchwardens and vestry in the election of Mr Nairn. But no such doubts affected the actions of the churchwardens. On Mr Nairn's death they proceeded as if they had undisputed powers of election. Richard Corpe, the vestry clerk, gave notice of a meeting of the vestry for the purpose of electing a new rector. Similarly, the town clerk of the Corporation had given notice of a meeting of the burgesses for the same purpose. It was predictable that at the meeting of the Corporation it would be agreed that the right of appointing the Rector of Poole was theirs. What was less predictable was that it was, at the same meeting, agreed to consider whether the Parsonage House should be taken down and the land thrown into the churchyard.

The great difference, however, between the election of the rector in 1767 and those of previous years was that the burgesses' man, Sam Fawconer, was a very good candidate. He had a very good personality and was a good preacher. By design or good judgement, he gave his probationary sermon just before the meeting of the Corporation to elect a rector and, far from resenting the choice of the burgesses, the churchgoers had waited outside the church after he had delivered his sermon and escorted him in a body to the Guildhall (now the new one in Market Street), and with their acclaim (and with their votes, they would afterwards claim) Sam Fawconer was elected Rector of Poole by universal consent.

This happy solution of the times' problems – and the first election to take place in the new Guildhall – left the fundamental disagreement between the burgesses and the vestry unresolved for the 21 happy years of Sam Fawconer's rectorship. The Corporation in 1769 agreed to prosecute those who owed tithes to Rev Fawconer. Galleries had earlier been built on the north and south aisles of the church to afford greater accommodation. In 1753 John Hayward had built the north gallery staircase and the galleries were again extended in 1785.

At the time of Mr Fawconer's election, Mr Scaplen and Mr Christopher Jolliffe were churchwardens. Church repairs were soon effected for the new rector and he was repaid the costs of his own repairs even when the Corporation had to raise a mortgage to do so, as in 1772 when they mortgaged Pitwines Close to repay Mr Fawconer £150. Moreover, the church itself was improved. In 1778 John Taylor painted the Lord's Prayer, the Creed and the Ten Commandments on the altar piece and the Corporation even paid for a new floor to be laid in their pew in the church.

Mr Fawconer was a friendly, jovial man as Mr Scaplen later remembered him. Coming into church one day he asked Mr Scaplen and his journeymen what they were doing. Mr Scaplen said, "I'm laying a new floor to the Corporation seat". "Lay a good foundation", joked Mr Fawconer, "for I think the Corporation is in a tottery condition!"

The Corporation, like the rest of Poole, was very favourably impressed by Mr Fawconer's ministry. In 1786, despite their earlier efforts to repair and renovate the old parsonage they decided to demolish it and put up a new house. On 1st March 1786 Josh Olive, the Mayor, William Spurrier, the senior bailiff, Thomas Hyde and Thomas Dean were appointed to inspect the parsonage house and report on its condition. On 26th June that year the Corporation ordered that £500 be borrowed on the security of the tithes of "Parkson and Longfleet for the rebuilding of the parsonage house and that the present Mayor, Samuel Bowden, Mr George Garland, Mr William Spurrier, Mr Benjamin Lester, Mr John Lester, Mr Peter Jolliffe, Mr James Seager and Mr John Skinner be a committee to superintend such Building". Mr Mark White Seager, one of the burgesses, lent the Corporation the necessary £500 on the 29th September and the work was commenced.

But Mr Fawconer had not lived to enjoy his new rectory for very long: he died in 1788. The popularity of Sam Fawconer is shown in that he was on his death the first rector to have a memorial erected in the church. His wife was allowed to put it there and she, on her death in 1818 established through her executors, the merchants George Garland, Christopher Spurrier and Peter Jolliffe, a fund to provide "sixpenny loaves" for poor old women. The bequest provided over 200 loaves each year which were distributed every Easter Monday at the church door by the minister and churchwardens to "the poor aged persons of the parish, among whom a preference is given to widows", and this Easter practice continued at least to the end of the old Corporation's existence.

On Mr Fawconer's death the town was back in the trauma of having another election on its hands. By this time everybody but the burgesses and the vestry, both of whom had definite and quite opposite views on the matter, were in genuine doubt as to who had the power to appoint the rector. Applicants for the curacy of the church on the death of Sam Fawconer were in great difficulty in how to act. Everybody they asked had a different opinion. Their sponsors, the vestry, the householders and the burgesses all told them that different sets of people had authority to elect the rector. Some of the applicants canvassed everybody in the town, even the many Quakers and Dissenters. The burgesses, however, resented applicants canvassing all the inhabitants. They took it as an affront to themselves that any others were encouraged to think they had any powers in the matter. The candidates were therefore not necessarily playing safe by canvassing everybody in the town.

The two front-runners in the 1788 election were Mr Richman, a nephew of the prominent burgess, George Olive, and a cousin of Joseph Olive, another burgess, and Mr William Davis.

Both of the candidates decided to canvass the whole town, so they both went from door to door in Poole in company with their burgess sponsors. With burgesses accompanying the candidates they were, of course, impliedly agreeing that the power of election did not remain solely with the burgesses and this made the position even more confused in the ordinary person's mind.

The two Olives, George Kemp and John Lester were among those supporting Mr Richman. These were powerful burgesses so that Mr Richman must have been favourite for the appointment. However, Mr Davis and his burgess supporters, William Spurrier and Thomas Dean, seeing the general canvass going against them, cleverly switched their canvass to that of the burgesses only and rested their candidature solely on the burgesses. Both candidates were so confused as to what they should do or tell the people whom they canvassed as to the legal position that each of them instructed lawyers to accompany them on their canvass. Mr Richman instructed a Mr Durnford and Mr Davis had the services of Mr Weston of Ringwood. Mr Weston had, of course, had experience of Poole's troubled elections of its rector, and it was probably on his advice that Mr Davis concentrated his campaign on the burgesses alone.

By this time Thomas Casely, the vestry's hero of previous struggles with the Corporation, had died and William Gaden had taken up the leadership of the vestry's struggle - and this despite his being the brother-in-law of William Spurrier, the Mayor, for he had married May Spurrier, the Mayor's sister.

The burgesses had fixed the 25th February 1788, as the date of their meeting to appoint the new rector. Mr Gaden and the vestry had made their plans ready for that meeting. They had decided that all those who paid scot and lot had a vote in the appointment of the rector and a great many of such people attended the meeting of the burgesses, all pledged to vote for Mr Richman.

William Gaden was ready for the Mayor's call for the vote and he quickly tendered his vote for Mr Richman. William Spurrier, the Mayor at the time, refused to accept it. This did not surprise the vestry members and, before the Mayor could announce the result of the votes of the burgesses, John Richman, a young attorney from Lymington who had been instructed by the vestry, asked the Mayor if he would then take the votes of the "commonalty". He carefully took the word from many of the Corporation's deeds and Charters which professed to give the Corporation's powers to "the Mayor, Bailiffs, Burgesses and Commonalty of the Town and County of Poole". William Spurrier's answer was to the point and quite brief. He merely said "No".

Even that answer had in no way surprised the inhabitants. The attorney then said, "Would you take *some* of the votes?", a question he had prepared beforehand to test whether the Mayor was distinguishing between mere inhabitants of Poole and those inhabitants who were paying scot and lot or those paying church or poor rates.

Members of the old Corporation, however, had little regard for such legal niceties. William Spurrier immediately replied, "No, not one of them!" and thereupon announced that Mr Davis had been elected the Rector of Poole.

The vestry were ready for this too. William Gaden immediately pushed himself forward to the Mayor and handed him a written formal objection which had already been signed by many of the inhabitants protesting formally that it had been "an undue election".

Once again a subscription list was opened to finance a case to be brought against the Corporation to establish that the burgesses had not the exclusive right of voting in the election of the rector and, in 1789, a writ was duly issued from the Chancery Court at the instigation of the members of the vestry.

The suit in Chancery was designed to establish the right of the parish at large to elect the minister of St James. They claimed that they had exercised this right in the past; that the original trustees had held the right on their behalf and not on behalf of the burgesses alone. The "informants" were William Gaden, George Kemp, Joseph Moore, John Symmonds, John Walls, Richard Miller, Richard Boorne, John Hunt, Joseph Pymer, Richard Daw, and Thomas Anstey.

It took until the Michaelmas term of 1791 before the cause came to trial before Lord Thurslow for it had to await the report of two commissions appointed by the court to examine witnesses and take evidence. The first commission, when they went to Poole, examined witnesses at the premises of John Stickland, "known by the sign of the New Antelope". In all, the commission examined 44 witnesses, and at the end of it, had a bigger series of contradictions on oath than could have been seen in even the Chancery Court for a very long time. Looking at the evidence dispassionately nearly 200 years later, however, it does seem to show that the petitioners had very little hard evidence to support them.

Their strongest point was, perhaps, the argument as to the frequent use of the word "commonalty" in the Corporation's documents and to make the point that the word "commonalty" meant nothing if it did not mean the ordinary people. But this point does not seem to have been argued strongly. The petitioners mainly rested their case on the assertion that William Street and Thomas Young were by inheritance the last survivors of the trustees of Durell's conveyance of 1692 but the lawyers who went from London to Poole to try to trace the heirs of these two men failed even in this.

Even the informants' own story of how they had elected previous rectors at vestry meetings could in no way be established, for Richard Corpe, the vestry clerk of those turbulent days of Mr Nairn's election in 1755 and of Sam Fawconer's election in 1767, had died in 1768. Richard Corpe's daughter, May Weston, had, on her father's death, gone to live with her two sons, James and Ambrose Weston in Fenchurch Street in London. When she had left Poole she had taken her father's books and papers with her, including all the old vestry books and papers. Her sons had put all these papers in the garrets of their home. In 1783 James Weston, finding "his garrets much incumbered with old books and papers", sold a great quantity of them to a cheesemonger who was in business near Fenchurch Street. (One can only speculate as to the likely resting place of these documents of Poole's turbulent history encompassing, rather unhygienically, the portions of cheese bought by the inhabitants of Fenchurch Street in the 1780s!) In the Hilary term of the courts in 1795 the suit of the "inhabitants" was finally dismissed with costs against the informants.

The rectors of Poole had rarely begun their ministries in Poole in an atmosphere conducive to peace and goodwill. The Rev William Davis was no exception. Although the Corporation granted him a three year lease of the tithes of Parkstone and Longfleet on the same terms as they had previously granted them to Sam Fawconer, William Davis, as is hardly surprising, found it impossible to continue in his appointment with his own churchwardens and vestry suing the burgesses for appointing him against their wishes. He had given up the unequal struggle in 1791 and resigned his appointment.

With the High Court case still proceeding therefore it was still in doubt as to who had the right to make the appointment of the next rector. The Rev Peter William Jolliffe MA, a young man of 25, was the leading applicant for the position of rector in 1791, but even he, with the support of his uncle, Peter Jolliffe, as well as that of Joseph Garland, Dr West and Capt Boorne went round canvassing the general public of Poole. When George Newman, an auctioneer, was approached for his vote by this impressive little posse, he said that he doubted whether parishioners would have a vote, whereupon the Rev Peter Jolliffe took a guinea wager with him that the inhabitants would be allowed a vote.

The Rev Jolliffe was later to get to know the burgesses better than to think that at such a time they would consider compromising their defence of the action in Chancery by allowing anyone but the burgesses to vote in his election. But, at least on this occasion, the burgesses, if they knew of it, did not allow the indiscretion of the Rev Jolliffe in his indiscriminate canvass to prejudice his case for, on 4th May 1791, they elected him as the next Rector of Poole. Naturally, it was the votes of the burgesses alone which were taken.

The Rev Peter William Jolliffe
who was Rector of Poole for 70 years.

Sterte House where the Rev Peter William Jolliffe lived and from which he walked
each morning to St James's.

173

INHABITANTS OF POOLE.

THE circumstances respecting my situation and property when I first came to Poole, and when I contracted to build your new Church, the loss which I and my Creditors have sustained in the Erection of that Building, (without meaning to reflect upon any one,) being altogether unknown to many of you and being I fear misunderstood by some; you will not I hope deem it intrusive in me to lay before you the real state of the case, for although I have been unfortunate, yet I wish to convince you that I never had an intention to injure any one.

The Cash which I brought with me to Poole and which I received afterwards before I began to build the Church, amounted to £1250 besides Household Furniture of the value of £80, and I have lost the whole of this sum (except about one hundred and fifty pounds which I lost by a fire at St. Johns) in building the Church, besides a heavy loss which my Creditors sustained; I owed no money whatever when I came to Poole, for I first started in business here; and I never paid any debts on account of my Father as it has been insinuated.

I am ready to verify these facts, and to prove the accuracy of the following statement, as far as concerns myself, and I presume the statement is correct as to the monies received by my Assignees or due to them.

THOS. BENHAM.

Dr.   **T. BENHAM** *for Cash Paid and Received on Account of* POOLE CHURCH AND TOWER,   Cr.

	£	s.	d.		£	s.	d.
Paid for Materials	5,990	19	4	Received of the Committee			
——— Wages	3,620	3	6½	and Churchwardens	9,711	0	0
—— Sundry Accounts	946	4	10	Balance of Cash paid more			
				than received	846	7	8½
	£ 10,557	7	8½		£ 10,557	7	8½

Abstract of Profit and Loss by the Contract.

	£	s.	d.		£	s.	d.
To Payments as above	10,557	7	8½	By Receipts as above	9,711	0	0
Sundry Bills now due				Cash my Assignees received			
to my Creditors	2,929	5	2½	from the Committee and			
				Churchwardens	1,041	14	3
				Ditto from Sale of Old			
				Materials, &c	372	0	0
				Balance lost	2,361	18	8
	£ 13,486	12	11		£ 13,486	12	11

MOORE AND SYDENHAM, PRINTERS POOLE.

Thomas Benham, the builder of St James's Church, got himself caught up in the quarrels of the town about the rebuilding of the Church and the costs involved. Criticisms of him were, apparently, not silenced by his loss on the contract, or even by his insolvency.

It was not until four years after the Rev Peter William Jolliffe's appointment that the Chancery case was decided and his long and successful reign as the Rector of Poole actually lasted longer than the old Corporation, so that, in the event, the long and costly litigation never did achieve an unchallenged election of a rector by the burgesses.

It was, though, in the Rev Peter Jolliffe's ministry that the new church of St James was built but, for most of his ministry, Peter Jolliffe did not live in the rectory, preferring his own house at Sterte. In 1819 Joseph Hannaford of Christchurch was engaged to report on the state of the old church of St James with John Kent of Southampton. Their report must have horrified the vestry. Apart from many structural and roof defects, the surveyors reported "we had occasion to take up some loose boarding which composed part of the floor of one of the pews, we observed several coffins with no other covering but loose boards, from which such an offensive smell arose that we were obliged to put the covering boards down again immediately, and on making some enquiry, we were informed there were many such places in different parts of the church, and which we are apprehensive is mistaken for the dampness of the water only. . . ."

The vestry vacillated as to what was to be done. First they agreed that much of the work should be done to make the building safe structurally. Then they decided the church must be rebuilt which, they decided would only cost £1,000 more than the cost of repairs if the outside was merely stuccoed and the tower left in position. Then they decided that the outside should be Portland stone at an extra cost of £370; then that the tower should be rebuilt, which added a further £2,000. This was too much for some of the Vestry who called a meeting to countermand this extravagance.

Their resolution was in similar terms to hundreds of such resolutions: ". . . it is not expedient at the present period of public distress when the deficiencies in the parochial rates are great beyond all precedent in consequence of the utter inability of the parishioners to pay them to burden the inhabitants with the expense of taking down and rebuilding the said tower . . .". The resolution was however defeated at the vestry meeting by 33 votes to 24. When the new tower was finally built and the estimate of £2,000 was exceeded the vote to disallow the extra cost of £730 was lost by an even smaller majority, and again, even in the rebuilding of the church, St James was engulfed in argument and bad feeling.

The foundation stone of the new church was laid at a masonic ceremony on 31st May 1819. The brethren assembled in the lodge room and the Provincial Grand Lodge was duly opened. Then the 200 brethren walked in procession to the Town Hall where they were joined by the Mayor and burgesses. The procession from Market Street to the site of the new building formed "an awfully grand and sublime procession, such as was never before witnessed in the Town and County of Poole". It was headed by two tilers with drawn swords and a band and followed, among others, by the visiting lodges, the Royal Arch Masons with staves, the tablet carried by the architect, the corn, wine and oil in silver goblets carried by three brethren and

WE do hereby give you notice that we are ready to Allot to you any one of the Pews in the North or South Gallery in the Parish Church of Saint James, in Poole, mentioned in the List below, at the Price to be paid by you set opposite to the number of the Pew which you wish to purchase, on condition of your giving us Notice in writing, to be delivered for us at the Dwelling House of the undersigned JOSEPH BARTER BLOOMFIELD, by Thursday Evening next at eight o'clock, that you accept the same at that price and that you surrender to us your present Pews or Sittings in the said Church, at and after the same Rate or Price which was given by you for such Seats or Sittings, and also on condition of your paying us the price of the Pew which you may so desire to purchase before twelve o'clock on the following day, and if you disapprove of purchasing any Seat or Pew at the price mentioned in the said list, we request you to make an offer to us by a note in writing signed by you and to be delivered for us at the Dwelling House of the undersigned J. B. BLOOMFIELD on or before Thursday next at eight o'clock in the evening, of the highest price which you will give for such Seat or Pew as you may wish to purchase.

If you decline or neglect to purchase at the price mentioned in the said list, or shall make an offer to purchase for a less Sum than we can get from another person, or shall neglect to give us any answer on or before Thursday next at eight o'clock in the evening at the place aforesaid, or shall on or before that time give such answer as shall not be decisive to the points aforesaid, or we can get a higher price than the sum which you may offer us as aforesaid, we shall proceed to sell all the Seats or Pews contained in the said list.

In case two or more persons shall accept our offer or make offers to purchase at the same price or sum we reserve to ourselves the liberty of making our election and giving such preference as may appear to us to be consistent with the order of priority and other circumstances.

The Purchasers of Seats or Pews are to hold them for three lives and be subject to the Rules and Regulations of the Church.

Number of Pews.	Prices.
No. 4.	£ 45.
8.	40.
9.	60.
16.	70.
17.	50.
24.	60.
25.	40.
32.	25.
49.	25.
56.	40.
57.	60.
61.	50.
65.	70.
72.	60.
73.	40.
80.	45.

Moore & Sydenham, Printers, Poole.

Pew rents were always a source of controversy but a source, also, of necessary money.

the treasurer of the Grand Lodge of England as well as by the Provincial Lodge officers.

On the laying of the stone "the Grand Honours were then given by the whole Craft" and the procession returned to the Guildhall which had been fitted up as a temporary church and so used until the opening of the new church, for divine service. The stone which was laid that day is now covered by the panelling of the church but is as follows:

Here stood the ancient Parish Church of St James
(whereof the Rev Peter William Jolliffe is the surviving Minister)
which having been consecrated to the worship of God
for many ages was taken down in order to erect a new Edifice
on its foundations
On the 31st day of May in the year of our Lord 1819 and in the
59th year of the reign of His Present Majesty George III the
most pious and best of men
The Chief Corner Stone of the New Church was laid
By William Williams Esq MP
Provincial Grand Master of the County of Dorset
Assisted by a numerous assemblage of the Ancient Fraternity
of Free and Accepted Masons
In the presence of Joseph White Orchard Esq
Mayor of the Town
The Magistrates
And a considerable part of the Body Corporate
Together with a large concourse of Inhabitants Unitedly ascribing
Glory to God in the Highest

In fact the stone was not laid by William Williams who, "through domestic trouble", was not even present at the ceremony. The stone was laid by the Deputy Provincial Grand Master, Thomas Parr, the Poole solicitor with offices in Fish Street and for whom the masons later erected a memorial in the church. (Thomas Parr was also the father of Robert Parr who was later the notorious town clerk of Poole.)

Six years ago St Peter's Anglican Church at Twillingate, Newfoundland, celebrated its 125th anniversary and then published a booklet in which it referred to St James, Poole. This is how it wrote of St James:

ST JAMES' CHURCH, Built 1142
Rebuilt 1819
Poole, Dorset, England

As early as 1794, Poole had 149 ships, seven of which were over 200 tons. These were probably the brigs which sailed to Newfoundland with general stores.

The close connection with Newfoundland is revealed by several babies born there but baptised in Poole Church.

The Church was rebuilt on the old foundations in 1819. The pine masts which support the roof, together with the massive roof timbers, came from Newfoundland, and the original slates lasted from 1819 to 1958. . . .

The photograph of the 1825 painting of the interior of St James also came from Newfoundland. It shows the original brass candelabra which George Garland gave to the church when it was first built and which were later sold by auction when gas lighting was installed in 1844. (John Slade then bought them at auction for £51 5s. 0d.,

An oil painting of 1825 of the interior of St James's. It shows the Cherub-head Chandeliers
and brackets for the candle lighting which George Garland gave to the Church.
When the Church lighting was converted to gas in 1844 John Slade
bought this 'Brasswork' and took it to Twillingate for use in St Peter's Church
where it was used until 1905.
The photograph of this oil painting came from St Peter's Anglican Church, Twillingate,
Newfoundland.

took them to Twillingate and presented them to St Peter's church where they were used until 1905.**)**

However, as it turned out, 1821 proved to be the last year in which the Corporation had any great involvement in the church or its rectory. The rebuilding of the church was complete early in 1821, and the use of the council chamber on the first floor of the Guildhall by the church had proved a great inconvenience to the burgesses. In early March that year they instructed Mr Orchard to tell the minister and churchwardens "to quit the Guildhall as a place of religious worship as soon as conveniently may be". This seemed to have had the desired effect for it was quickly decided to open the church on Easter Monday that year.

The opening of the church was the subject of a formal record being placed in the Corporation's books and, apart from a later formal inquiry into whether the Corporation was liable to pay the £12 16s. 0d. as directed by Ettricke's will, it was the last entry in the Corporation's record book relating to St James. It was:

ON EASTER MONDAY, 23rd April, 1821, being the Anniversary of the Birth Day of his Majesty George the Fourth and St George's Day.

The New Parish Church of St James in this Town and County was opened for Divine Worship, which interesting Event was celebrated by a public Breakfast consisting of between two and three hundred persons, at the Guildhall, provided at the Expense of the Corporation, who are Patrons of the said Church.

After Breakfast a Procession (composed of the Corporate Body and many other Inhabitants, preceded by a Number of distinguished Clergymen from the Neighbourhood in their Canonicals, and followed by the Friendly Societies of the Town, and also attended by the Peace Officers, the Sergeants at Mace with their Maces, Music playing, Town Guns firing, and Colours flying &c. &c.) took place to the church, where Divine Service was performed by the following Clergymen in the presence of a very crowded Congregation, estimated at between four and five thousand Persons.

The Prayers were read in a most impressive Manner by the Revd Samuel Clark of Compton in the County of Somerset, a Burgess of this Corporation. The Communion Service was conducted by the Revd C. Bowle, Master of Arts, of Wimborne Minster, the Official – After which the Revd P. W. Jolliffe, Master of Arts, also a Burgess of this Corporation and Minister of the Parish delivered with great Pathos a very appropriate and excellent discourse from 4 Chapr of John and 24 Verse.

Public Worship being concluded, the Procession returned under the salute from the Town Guns to the Guildhall (to which they were invited by the Mayor who had provided Cake and Wine for the Occasion at his own expence) and evinced their Loyalty by drinking his Majesty's Health, with various other Toasts adapted to the occasion.

A Ball, Fire Works &c and other demonstrations of Joy closed the proceedings of this eventful Day.

        Geo. W. Ledgard. Mayor.

It was as well that the burgesses apparently did so well for the opening service of the new church for, though they could have hardly suspected it, it was the last substantial act they were ever to perform as its patrons. The Rev Peter Jolliffe outlived the old Corporation. It was dissolved by the Municipal Corporations Act, 1835, and the new council which inherited the rights and patronage of the church sold these rights in 1845 in a desperate attempt to raise money.

However, the church still stands as a proud memory to the old Poole people who fought for the right to attend the services in the church, to take part in its services and to have a say in the church's affairs. On the walls of the church are commemorated some of the merchants of the town who once made Poole prosperous and famous and, in the records of the church and in its massive roof timbers and supports, it still commemorates Poole's great involvement in the fishing and trade of Newfoundland.

The rectory, too, still stands in its grounds beside the church, a challenge to the modern rectors of Poole to make it reasonably habitable to accord with our present day needs of space, comfort and heating – but at least no longer susceptible to the interference of the Corporation.

The Rectors of Poole
(occupants of the three parsonage houses and rectories of St James, Poole)

1529	William Birte	1692	William Churchey
1546	Thomas Hancock	1702	Daniel Hyde
1554	Thomas Long	1705	John Conant
1557	Simon Berwyke	1720	Christopher Derby
1559	John Seywarde	1734	Richard Derby
1566	Matthew Haviland	1748	John Culme
1570	Robert Ryckman	1755	William Nairn
1580	Robert Fossey	1767	Samuel Fawconer
1581	Richard Marcan	1788	William Davis
1582	William Hiley	1791	Peter William Jolliffe
1611	Nicholas Jeffrey	1861	Alfred Wilkinson
1624	Henry Anketel	1868	John A Lawson
1630	Swithin Cleeves	1905	Reginald Fawkes
1642	Josiah White	1910	Henry L Phillips
1643	John Gundy	1924	Ceredig Egerton-Williams
1645	– Owfield	1931	Bernard Herklots
1647	John Hadderley	1935	Edward C Harris
1650	Thomas Thackham	1954	George H W Bevington
1667	Samuel Hardy	1960	Bryn B Bell
1682	Robert Howson	1968	Thomas L Livermore
1685	John Russell	1975	John Potter
1691	James Hanne		

Appendix

Home-thoughts, from abroad

Exploits, many years ago, showing on the left the house of Andrew Pearce II, its store, and waterfront.

Andrew Pearce at the Harbour Control Office, Botwood.

ANDREW PEARCE

Botwood, Newfoundland, Canada.

Andrew Pearce, now 70 years old, is the fifth consecutive "Andrew Pearce" of the family. He is the great great grandson of the Andrew Pearce who was joint manager with John Colborne of Sturminster of the merchant firm of John Colborne & Co of Poole. The original Andrew Pearce came to Poole from Piddleton, Dorset, and had four sons, Elias, Andrew, Joseph and Frederick, and three daughters, Amy, Audrey and Elizabeth.

The family of the present Andrew Pearce lived for over a hundred years at Exploits on Burnt Island, Newfoundland, some 15 miles from the island of Twillingate. In 1960 the present Andrew Pearce moved from Exploits to Botwood where, still involved with ships, he was for 37 years a harbour pilot.

Andrew Pearce's family often talked of the early days of the family in Newfoundland and wondered what had happened to the other Pearces who remained at Poole or Piddleton. What happened, he wonders, to Joseph (who was so very sea-sick on a journey to and from Newfoundland) and to his sisters, Amy, Audrey and Elizabeth Pearce, who were probably married and stayed in Poole when the others left to live in Newfoundland?

The schooner 'Mountaineer' nearing Leghorn, John Tilsed, Master.

CYRIL T. TAYLOR

19617 Seventh Place South, Seattle, Washington 98148, USA.

Cyril Taylor's great, great grandfather's brother was John Ross Taylor, one of whose butcher's shops we showed in photograph 178 in *An Album of Old Poole*. His own great great grandfather, Henry Taylor, was a Poole ship's captain and lived at Longfleet in 1871, and had previously worked for the Slades, merchants of Poole. In 1858 he had been boatswain on the *Mountaineer* of Poole which was pictured in *The Pride of Poole*.

Cyril Taylor is writing a book of the history of his ancestor, Henry Taylor and his family, and came to England this autumn to gather material for his book.

He isn't the only Poole Taylor in the USA. He has an uncle, Ralph Taylor, who was born in Poole in 1904 and who emigrated with his parents to America in 1913. There is, too, in Washington a cousin, Henry Robertson, who left Poole in 1909.

Cyril Taylor would appreciate help in locating any business records, photographs and paintings for his book.

New Harbour, Trinity Bay, Newfoundland. George Garland's vessels often sailed from here.

FREDERICK WILLIAM NEWHOOK
Topsail Road, St John's, Newfoundland, Canada.

Catherine Pynn's family were one of the very earliest settlers in Newfoundland. In fact, the land which she inherited from the Pynns had a title which actually predated the time when anyone, other than the Crown, was officially entitled to own any land in Newfoundland. Catherine Pynn married a Poole man, Captain Taverner, and her sister Susanna married a Bristol man, Conway Heighington, who owned property on the south side of Harbour Grace. Conway and Susanna Heighington retired to Bristol and when Susanna died in 1834 she left her share of the Pynn and Heighington estates in Newfoundland to her nieces, the two daughters of her sister Catherine Taverner.

Meanwhile, however, the two Taverner daughters, Sarah and Susanna had each married one of two brothers, both ship's captains of Poole. Sarah Taverner had married Thomas Lander, and her sister Susanna had married John Lander. Each of the sisters had only one child. Sarah called her daughter Sarah after herself and it was this daughter Sarah who had, in 1831, married Charles Newell Newhook, who was Frederick William Newhook's great great grandmother.

The other sister, Susanna, called her daughter Louisa Maria, but the family did not stay in Newfoundland long. John Lander brought his wife and daughter to live in East Street in Poole where he was made harbour master. He died in the 1850's and Mrs Susanna Lander and her daughter Louisa, who had not married, moved to a house in Green Lane.

It was here at her house in Green Lane that Louisa Lander instructed Mr Dickinson, solicitor and part-time town clerk of Poole, to make a will for her which was witnessed by Charles Lisby, his chief clerk, and who was himself later town clerk. Louisa Lander died in 1892 and left her interests in the Newfoundland estates to her cousin, Sarah Newhook, of New Harbour, Trinity Bay, Newfoundland. She also left to her cousin Sarah two 18th century silver mugs, one of which was engraved with the Lander monogram, and which is now in the Newfoundland museum.

Hubert Forsey at the terminus of the Trans-Canada Highway in 1974.

HUBERT FORSEY

St. John's, Newfoundland, Canada.

Hubert Forsey was born in Fogo, Newfoundland, in 1892. His great great grandfather, Samuel Forsey, came from Devon; Elizabeth, his great great grandmother's parents probably came from Poole. Samuel Forsey had emigrated to Newfoundland in 1786 as an apprentice to a Newfoundland planter in Fogo called John Banks.

Hubert Forsey's mother was a friend of "Lady Waterman" of Poole in Fogo and, when the blueberries were ripe, little Hubert, in about 1900, would carry Mrs Waterman's "basket of goodies" on an expedition of blueberry picking. "Lady Waterman was a very refined and cultured lady, and kind and loving to everybody", but later she left Fogo and went to live in Florida.

Hubert was a fisherman in Fogo but, in between, was in the Navy in the Great War of 1914–18. Now, "like the fish my great grandfather caught", he has "ended up in St John's". There he still thinks of Fogo and the other Forseys in Fogo, icebound in their deep-water port for five months a year.

He still wonders, too, about Jane Jolliffe, the granddaughter of James Jolliffe, who emigrated from Poole to Fogo in 1813. Jane Jolliffe received a letter from a firm of Poole solicitors in 1926 telling her that she would hear something to her advantage if she could show that she was the daughter of James Jolliffe. The local preacher took this letter with him when he was going on a visit to St John's so that he could ask his lawyers there to reply on behalf of Jane Jolliffe. The minister, though, had his wallet stolen from his jacket in St John's and no reply was ever sent to the solicitors, for no one could remember their name or address.

He and his family have often taken communion in the Anglican Church of St Andrews, Fogo, where the solid silver chalice engraved "Presented by Slade & Co., Poole, England." is still in use today.

Index

SEVEN YEARS' WAR 1756-63 91

SEYMOUR Alfred MP for Totnes, brother of Lady Tichborne 38, 41

SEYMOUR Henry Danby MP for Poole 33, 38

SEYMOUR FAMILY 26

SHAFTESBURY Earl of 99, 126

SILLY COVE Newfoundland later called WINTERTON 90, 121

SKINNER John Poole merchant, Sheriff 1758 and Mayor 1769-70 169

SKUTT Allen Mayor 1677

SMITH Harry Peace (quoted) 141

SMITH Admiral Thomas 127

SMITHBY Thomas purchases rights of the Rectory 155, 156

SNOW William last Prior of Bradenstoke, later Dean of Bristol 151

SOUZA Luiz Antonio de agent for Colborne in Portugal 144

SPRATT Samuel 141

SPURRIER Amy daughter of Christopher and Amy Spurrier 19

SPURRIER Ann widow of Timothy Spurrier 16

SPURRIER Ann daughter of Timothy and Ann Spurrier 16

SPURRIER Christopher son of William Spurrier, MP Bridport 1820, died 1876 aged 93 16, 18, 19, 23, 25, 169

SPURRIER Captain Christopher officer in the Royal Navy 18

SPURRIER John sailmaker at Poole 18

SPURRIER Mary wife of Walter Spurrier 13

SPURRIER Mary daughter of Ann Spurrier 16

SPURRIER Mary sister of William Spurrier and wife of William Gaden 170

SPURRIER Thomas Henry Lester Water Bailiff 1829-31 23

SPURRIER Timothy Senr Sheriff 1721, Mayor of Poole 1722, 1725, 1730-31, died 1756 14, 126

SPURRIER Timothy Junr Sheriff 1739, Mayor of Poole 1747 and 1751 14

SPURRIER Walter son of Timothy Spurrier 13

SPURRIER William Inspects Rectory 1786, Mayor 1784, 1786-87 16, 25, 169, 171

SPURRIER William Naval officer in Newfoundland Rebuked by House of Commons later for interference with an election writ 18

SPURRIER William Jubber Poole merchant 18, 22

SPURRIER FAMILY Trading at St Mary's Bay, Newfoundland 14

SPURRIER, JOLLIFFE & SPURRIER Poole firm bankrupt in 1830 22

STEELE Isaac 139

STERTE Rector Rev P W Jolliffe resided at Sterte House 175

STICKLAND John landlord of "New Antelope" New Street 171

STONE Thomas agent for Lester in Newfoundland 95

STONE COTTAGE Wimborne 114, 119

STREET William a trustee of St James's Church 172

STRONG John Sheriff 1790, Mayor 1805-06, 1808-09 99

STUART Maj-Gen Charles MP for Poole 113

STURT Humphrey Charles 19

STYRING Frederick Brewer Sheriff 1855, Mayor of Poole 1866, 1875, 1887 80

SUCHET Marshal French commander in Spain 73

SUKEY (ship) 90

SUSAN (ship) captured by the French 90, 100

SWETLAND John Poole builder of Mansion House for Isaac Lester 94

SWIFT (ship) 113

SYMMONDS John 171

TAVERNER Jacob Newfoundland merchant 90

TAVERNER Mary wife of Samuel White 1647-1720 131

TAVERNER Rachel wife of Francis Lester 85

TAVERNER Sarah wife of John Masters 122

TAVERNER Sarah wife of Thomas Lander 184

TAVERNER Susanah wife of John Lander 184

TAVERNER William Newfoundland merchant 55, 85, 121

TAYLOR Cyril T 183

TAYLOR Henry Poole ship's captain 183

TAYLOR John paints altar piece for St James's Church 1778 169

TAYLOR John Ross a butcher in Poole 183

TAYLOR Ralph 183

THACKHAM Thomas intruded Rector, died 1667 158

THOMAS (ship) 90, 133

THOMAS & REBECCA (ship) 146

THOMPSON James brother of Sir Peter Thompson 56, 58

THOMPSON Captain Peter succeeds to Sir Peter Thompson's property 1770 62

THOMPSON Sir Peter FRS FSA 1698-1770 Hamburg merchant, antiquary and book collector, High Sheriff of Surrey and MP 55, 56, 62, 121, 124, 127, 133

THURLOW Edward 1st Baron 1731-1806 later Lord Chancellor 171

TICHBORNE Alfred 11th Baron Tichborne 30

TICHBORNE Benjamin brother of Henry 27

TICHBORNE Edward see DOUGHTY

TICHBORNE Henry 27

TICHBORNE Henrietta Felicité mother of Roger 30, 34, 38

TICHBORNE James brother of Edward Doughty 25, 27

TICHBORNE Joseph 50

TICHBORNE Roger Charles Doughty son of James Tichborne 27, 29, 30, 31, 42, 47

TICHBORNE DEFENCE FUND 45

TITO George shipbuilder, Mayor of Poole 1755 and 1771 127, 166, 168

TRADE AND PLANTATIONS Commissioners 13

TRENCHARD Henry MP for Poole 1688 159

TRENCHARD Thomas MP for Poole 1690 158, 159

TRINITY Newfoundland 90, 115

TRITON (ship) 112

TULLOCH Captain skipper of the "General Wolfe" 72

191

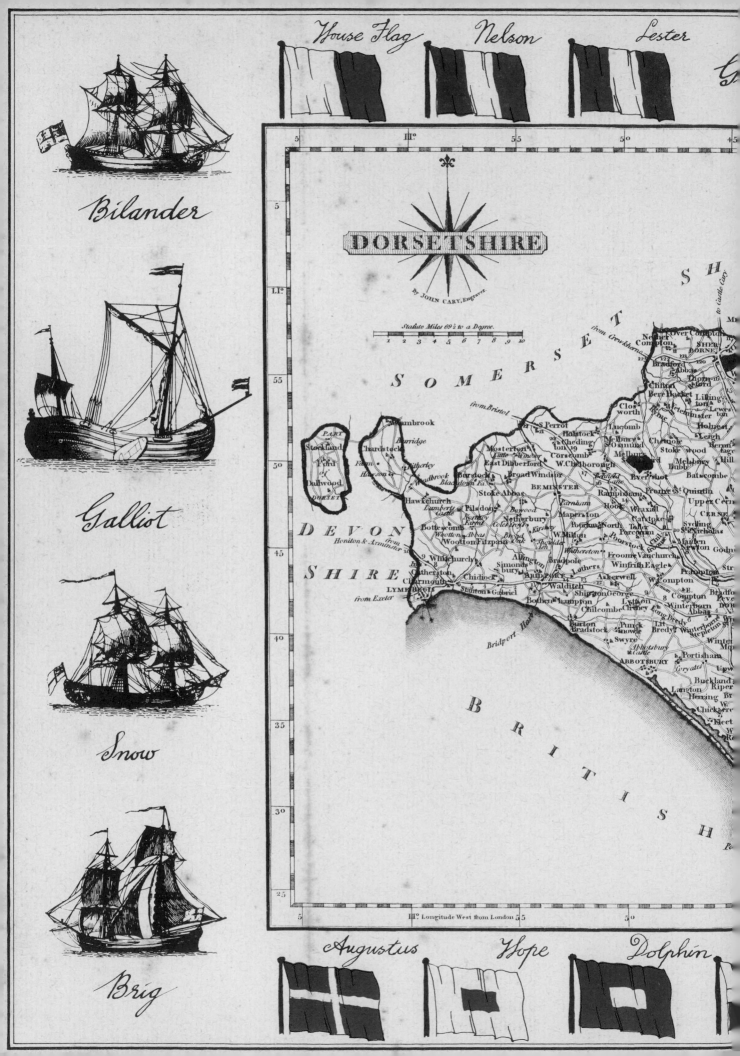

Bilander

Galliot

Snow

Brig

House Flag

Nelson

Lester

Augustus

Hope

Dolphin

✶

DORSETSHIRE

By JOHN CARY, Engraver.

Statute Miles 69½ to a Degree.

S O M E R S E T

SH

D E V O N

S H I R E

B R I T I S H

III°. Longitude West from London